BACK ON MY BIKE

How Cycling Transformed
My Life after Sixty

TOM EASTHAM

1

One damp April day in 2018, on completing my first proper bicycle ride for over three decades, I scarcely imagined I'd end up writing this book a couple of years later. For one thing the bike was wedged under my wife's car, with me still attached to it, as I'd turned onto our slippery driveway too quickly, so eager was I to dump the dratted machine in the garage, tear off my soggy gear, and jump in the shower.

"You should have power-washed the drive the last time I reminded you," my wife Sarah said on my revealing a square inch of lightly grazed elbow skin.

"Is that all you can say?" I moaned. "I could have broken something."

She tittered. "Not with all your padding."

I slapped my ancient tracksuit bottoms. "What padding?"

"All that fat you've been carrying for donkey's years."

I thrust back my shoulders and breathed in. "What fat?"

She lifted my old, totally permeable cagoule and a couple more layers, then grasped two fistfuls of excess adipose. "This fat. I'll grant that you haven't got much of a belly, but like Simon said, your sedentary lifestyle is taking its toll and it's high time you did something about it."

Simon is Sarah's boss, my dentist, and a long-time friend. If your missus of thirty-five years is a dental assistant and hygienist the chances are that even sixty-year-old gnashers will be in good shape, but during my last check-up, Simon – after rattling off the usual incomprehensible mantra as he tapped each tooth – had seen fit to extend his inspection to the rest of me. I was a flaccid specimen, he opined, and ought to resume the jogging I used to do once or twice a week.

"Makes my knees ache."

"Tennis then. Call one of your old partners."

"Ivan took up golf and Jim emigrated."

"Walking."

"I'm walking around that damned hotel all day long."

When he grinned I swear his upper canines twinkled. "You know what I'm going to say next."

I grimaced. "On your bike, mate. You'll not see me on one again, not on the roads nowadays."

He sighed as he closed a drawer full of sharp implements. "Ah, I'll never forget that ride we did when you and Sarah were still courting."

Sarah exited stage left, having heard this particular scratched record innumerable times. I rose from the still reclined chair and made for the coat hooks.

"You were as fit as a butcher's dog and I was just starting out."

"Yes. Must be off now, Simon."

"On that old Raleigh bike with only five gears."

"Hmm."

"And you on that super Italian racing bike."

"Which I sold shortly afterwards, yes. Look, Simon, in cycling terms we passed like shi... bikes in the night. I was fed up to the back teeth of trying to fit it in around work, while it was all new to you."

"And I've never looked back. Oh, you haven't seen my new S-Works yet," he said, referring to his latest ten-grand steed.

"No, you must wheel it round for dinner one night."

"Ha, yes." He peered into the tiny basin by the chair. "That's to say, no, not that one," I believe he muttered.

"I was joking. I've seen the evolution of your bike collection. I like them, from an aesthetic point of view, but you'll not get one between my legs, not with the state of the traffic these days."

"Bah, traffic! Always the same excuse. You know full well that from Fulwood you can be on the lanes within a matter of minutes," he said, referring to the pleasant neighbourhood to the north of Preston where we both resided.

"Cyclists get killed every day," I whined.

"So do motorists and pedestrians and... and camel drivers, I imagine. It's just a question of using your loaf and reducing the risk. How about this Saturday?"

I gulped. "What?"

"Dinner at yours."

"All right, but just bring Sue."

His canines glinted again, then he escorted me to the door. "You'll be retiring soon. I can't spare Sarah just yet, so you'll need something to keep yourself occupied."

"I've got plent–" I began, but he shoved me into the waiting room and beckoned his next patient.

During that fateful dinner I was waiting for the topic of cycling to rear its irksome head, because whenever it arose at our periodic get-togethers it was generally three against one. Simon's slim wife Sue did leisurely rides most summer weekends with a few friends, and while Sarah's old bike with its quaint little shopping basket had been gathering dust for some time, during the last couple of years she'd begun to side with Simon in his tiresome quest to get me back on the road.

A little historical data may be appropriate at this point. Between the ages of fifteen and twenty-seven I must have ridden close to 80,000 miles, although there were no cycle computers back then to set one's mileage in stone. After tootling around the Fylde flatlands with school friends for a while, I joined a local cycling club and was soon able to complete their long Sunday rides without arriving home in a state of total exhaustion. During my teenage years covering great distances was what appealed to me most and every summer I went youth hostelling and cycle camping whenever I got the opportunity. On achieving mediocre A-Level grades, partly due to preferring cycling to revision, I decided to forsake further studies and take a job at a Preston hotel.

At first my work was just a means to an end and I spent much of my free time on my bike. After completing a local ten-mile time trial surprisingly quickly for a lad accustomed to hundred-mile slogs, I turned my attention to racing and ended up clocking respectable times in events over ten, twenty-five and fifty miles. I also tried my hand at mass-start road races where – I like to think – my tactical naivety prevented me from achieving better results, for in a race of that type one must keep one's powder dry until the crucial moves are made, rather than powering along at the front of the bunch just for the hell of it, as I tended to do.

At work, although none too keen on doing overtime, I was always happy to help out wherever I was needed. By the age of twenty-two I'd become familiar with most aspects of hotel work, from scrubbing porridge-encrusted pans to planning small hospitality events, so when I was offered the post of duty manager at a large Blackpool hotel I jumped at the chance to cross the vaguely defined barrier between perennial dogsbody and management material. This entailed a longish commute, frequent sleepovers, and more hours, so the demise of my cycling began about then. My mileage declined, my race times worsened, and in addition to my onerous job I'd met my first and last serious girlfriend.

Sarah couldn't understand my despondency at no longer being able to do sub-hour twenty-five-mile time trials at the drop of a hat and I still vaguely remember a pertinent conversation which took place during the Moscow Olympics, when Coe and Ovett were thrilling the nation. It went something like this.

"Oh, it's all right for them, with all the time in the world to train, but how the hell can I get near my best times on a measly 150 miles a week?"

Perplexed look. "But what does it matter, Tom? You're not a professional athlete like them. Just go out on your bike when you can and enjoy your rides."

Snort. "It's not about enjoying myself."

Raised brows. "No?"

"No, it's about... oh, I don't know what it's about. I should have carried on touring, but the racing sort of sucked me in and I can't just ride for fun any more. I hate it when people beat me who I used to pass like a flash, but they don't work fifty-odd hours a week. I might just hang up my bikes for a while."

She twiddled her engagement ring, then squeezed my hand. "I don't want you to pack in cycling because of me, Tom. I know it's as important to you as the violin is to me, and we mustn't give up our interests."

Sarah kept her part of the bargain, because she still performs with a local string quartet and is occasionally invited to play ninth or tenth fiddle in a larger orchestra, but the writing was on the wall for my cycling aspirations. Although I plodded on for another few years, the fire was gone and it was almost a relief when I finally sold or gave away every item of cycling gear I possessed. Being knocked off by a car shortly after that ride with Simon didn't help, and although I wasn't badly hurt, after I'd packed it in I began to see danger lurking on every road and street along which I drove.

For any non-cyclists who may be reading this I ought to point out that cycling looks more dangerous from the driver's seat than from the saddle. On the bike a competent rider's senses are always tuned to detect danger, such as a car door about to open or a lunatic preparing to overtake on a blind bend, and he or she knows when to brake, swerve or even leave the road in order to keep body and bike in one piece.

So it was that as traffic increased I thanked my lucky stars that I was no longer exposing my fragile limbs to the perils of the road. I'd had a good run, but my wife and my career were far more important than pedalling pointlessly on, and when our son David was born in 1986 I swore to steer him towards safer sports, convinced that the post-millennial roads would be a veritable death-trap for cyclists. (David now lives near London, works in the film industry, sings in a highly regarded choir, swims like a fish, and has barely turned a pedal in his life.)

Back to the dinner. While we were scoffing Sarah's delicious pasta bake and sipping white wine, Simon spoke about selling his dental practice in two years' time. By then he and his faithful assistant would both be sixty and happy to call it a day. Simon, being an independent operator, was pretty loaded, which was just as well, given his serious bike habit, while Sarah and I were looking forward to a comfortable retirement, thanks to the substantial pension payments we'd been making for almost twenty years. Sue had already retired from her teaching job and was spending much of her time doing charity work in the town. When she told us once more how satisfying she found it, I suspected the conversation was subtly wending its way towards the two years of solo retirement I would enjoy before Sarah also joined the ranks of the leisured classes.

"I'm not going to wind the practice down though," Simon chipped in. "As I want to be in a strong position when I come to sell it."

Here it comes, I thought.

"Ah, yes, two more years of grafting, then I'll be a full-time cyclist, ha ha." He glanced at Sue. "That's to say, when we haven't got anything else to do."

She smiled. "Don't worry, you'll have plenty of time to indulge your passion." She looked at Sarah. "We might even get a tandem, but I've suggested borrowing one first to see if I get the hang of it."

"Good idea. I wouldn't fancy riding along looking at Tom's fat bum."

I was convinced they were planning a pincer movement, but I had an apt response ready, as I'd arranged to play golf with a colleague the following weekend. I secretly detested golf and all that went with it, but by declaring that I might take it up I hoped to quash the pro-cycling pep talk that was coming my way.

Simon gazed at me, sipped his wine, then asked Sarah how the music was going. She told him her ensemble were rehearsing Schubert's String Quartet No. 14, 'Death and the Maiden', which they hoped to perform at a few small regional gatherings that summer. As Sue and Simon aren't as musically inept as me, she went into some detail about her part in the forty-minute piece and before I knew it we were drinking coffee and Simon had begun to yawn, a sure sign that he wished to get his beauty sleep before his Sunday ride.

Out on the driveway Simon and Sarah indulged in a little shop talk while Sue and I gazed at the stars.

"I'm playing golf next weekend," I told her.

"Are you? How nice."

"Yes, I might take it up when I retire."

I think she winced at the moon. "Yes, a lot of blokes do." She smiled. "Still, if you're ever at a loose end, you could always come and lend a hand at the charity."

"Er, yes, I could."

"Would you prefer to help recovering drug addicts or former convicts?"

Neither, I thought, but she had pricked my conscience a bit. "We'll see. I might do something to help... someone."

She chuckled. "No pressure, but you will find that you've got an awful lot of time on your hands."

Then they were gone and Sarah was locking the door.

"You look befuddled, Tom."

"Eh? I was sure you were going to... oh, never mind."

I soon began to lay the table for breakfast, one of my many domestic duties.

"I'm going up."

"Won't be long, love."

She paused on the stairs. "Oh, just check the garage door, will you? It didn't seem to click shut properly earlier."

"All right." I headed towards the front door.

"From the inside," she said sharply.

I sniffed the air, having smelt a rat, but my wife had scurried up the stairs like a large, mischievous rodent. On opening the door into the garage I saw that the strip lighting was on and the usually empty oblong of concrete was occupied by two old chairs. Upon one chair there lay a pile of clothing topped by a fluorescent helmet, while against the other a shiny bicycle had been balanced, pointing toward the driveway, poised for action.

I groaned, flicked off the lights, and put a security door between me and that tantalising sight. After a couple of turns around the kitchen table it struck me that the gleaming mount was none other than Simon's titanium-framed dream-machine, once his pride and joy, but now only the fourth or fifth best of his dozen or so bikes. I began to climb the stairs, intending to give Sarah a piece of my mind for conspiring behind my back, but I came to a halt on the third step. As Simon had chosen to lend me such a marvellous bike, the least I could do was to take a good look at it, so I re-entered the garage and began to circle it from a safe distance. As I said, I still found bikes pleasing on the eye and this one was a really beauty. Unlike the generally gaudy carbon frames which most folk prefer these days, the plain titanium with no lettering whatsoever looked sleek and dignified under the bright lights. The components were all top of the range and the wheels appeared to be a featherweight pair with about twenty sturdy spokes and deepish rims. I approached and touched one of the shifters, mechanical marvels operating both brakes and gears which I'd never tried, before grasping the frame and lifting the bike.

"Christ, it's light," I muttered, before spinning the front wheel. "Smooth as silk."

I propped the bike carefully against the chair and made for the door. With my hand on the light switches I looked over my shoulder and sighed. I pictured the network of flat lanes to the north-west of Preston which were still stamped upon my memory. Had Simon lent me his well-used touring bike or the cheap aluminium-framed racer which had succeeded that first Raleigh I could have driven either one round to his house the next day and said, 'Nice try, mate,' but as he'd entrusted me with a four-grand bike upon which he'd covered thousands of miles before finally succumbing to the lure of ultra-light carbon, the least I could do was to go for a short spin on it.

I decided to do that. In return for his kindness I'd brave the roads for an hour, before cleaning the bike and regretfully telling him that although it was superb, cycling still wasn't for me. I tried the helmet for size and found that it fit my big head perfectly. I sniffed the foam pads inside it and they smelt new. I began to inspect the clothing. I'm a shade over six feet tall and, despite my fatty padding, not overly corpulent, while Simon is a wiry five foot ten, so in theory his cast-off clothing wouldn't quite fit me. The lycra tights and shorts looked used and would probably stretch that little bit further, as would the fingerless gloves, but the long-sleeved jacket with go-faster fluorescent stripes smelt as new as the helmet. My suspicions aroused, I pulled a pair of shoes from the bottom of the pile. They were size eleven, not too flashy, and had been fitted with cleats for the double-sided SPD pedals on the bike. On examining one of these undoubtedly new shoes a small Allen key fell out, presumably to use on the cleats if I needed to adjust them. There was also a little bag to attach to the saddle, in which I found two spare inner tubes, tyres levers, a compact multi-tool, and the tiniest pump I'd even seen. I noticed a nifty cycle computer on the handlebars too, alongside a small light which matched the rear one attached to the seat post.

"He's thought of everything," I murmured. "And I doubt he's worked alone."

After one last look at the bike I locked the door and headed up to bed, where I found Sarah reading a novel, something she rarely did after our Saturday soirées. I stood staring at the book cover until her blue eyes peeped over the top.

"What's up with you? Have you seen a ghost or something?"

"Yes, a ghostly vision from the past. So, who's been wasting their money then?"

"What money?"

"New shoes, new jacket, new helmet, new saddle pack and... whatever else is new."

"Oh, Simon bought them and I paid him."

"Foolish expenditure, I'm afraid."

"I thought it was the least I could do."

"Why?"

"Well, he's given you the bike, hasn't he?"

I gasped. "He's *given* me the bike?"

"Yes, he always felt it was a tad too big for him, and you know what a perfectionist he is."

I shook my head till my cheeks wobbled. "But... but, that's crazy. I mean, incredibly generous, but crazy."

"Oh, I don't know. I protested too, till he reminded me how much money I've helped him to make over the years, then I backed down. Of course you can only keep it if you use it. That's the sole condition of ownership."

I sat on the bed and pulled off my slippers, as we never dressed too formally for our dinners. "The pair of you have steered me into a corner." I heard her book close. "But that doesn't mean I'm going to be riding out of it and into that infernal traffic."

"Interestingly put, but Simon tells me that most of the lanes are as quiet as ever. He's given you the bike for a reason, you know."

"You may have read my mind, love. I was just wondering why on earth he's prepared to make such a great sacrifice. He loves that bike, even though he no longer rides it much, so why attempt to give it to me?"

She reached over and ruffled my closely cropped grey hair. "Because he *knows*."

I turned around. "He *knows* what, pray?"

He knows that you'll enjoy cycling if only you'll make the effort to do a couple of rides. He knows it'll be a great thing for you to do once you leave that lousy hotel behind."

I bridled. "It's the best hotel in Morecambe, largely thanks to me."

"Lousy in the sense that running it has tired you out for the last six years, even more than the other places you've turned around."

"At least I'll be ending my career on a high."

"That's true, and I'm glad, but I'm worried about the great big hole that retirement's going to leave in your life."

I told her I'd have plenty to do, like sprucing up the garden, repairing the ailing shed, and doing a spot of decorating. "And reading more, and... and doing brisk walks."

She sighed. "It won't be nearly enough, Tom. A man with your energy needs a serious hobby, ideally one which will challenge you physically, or do you want to turn into one of those… podgy potterers we see so many of on the estate?"

I pictured the neighbours to our left. They put in more hours in front of the box than a prisoner in solitary – with a TV set – and on fine days they laboured listlessly or loafed in their garden.

"Take Brian and Celia, for instance," Sarah said.

"I was just… what about them?"

She shrugged. "I think he's sixty-six. Retired about three years ago."

I pictured the corpulent former postie more closely and didn't like what I saw. Brian wasn't lazy or stupid, but he appeared to be entering a semi-vegetative state. I undressed briskly and went to brush and floss my teeth. After hopping into bed I promised Sarah that I'd go for a ride the very next day.

She gave me a peck on the cheek. "Good."

"Happy now?"

"Yes, and so will you be."

2

Any especially attentive readers may be wondering why, after being gifted a decent set of cycling clothes, I instead went for my maiden ride in ancient tracksuit bottoms and a crummy old cagoule. I did in fact shove my flabby legs into the lycra tights and zip up the go-faster jacket, but once I'd strapped on the helmet and stepped into the shoes I felt like such an imposter that I changed into more suitable clothing for a man about to pedal along at a snail's pace for a few miles. It being a Sunday morning, I expected to see plenty of proper cyclists heading for the lanes and I didn't want them to mistake me for one of them. No, far better for them to believe I was a scruffy old sod on a stolen bike than have them wondering why I was floundering along at a pathetic ten miles an hour, if that, although I did don the padded shorts under my baggy trackies and had to wear the shoes because the pedals were too small to be used with trainers. I donned the hi-vis helmet for safety's sake, of course, but went gloveless, as it wasn't too cold and almost certainly wouldn't rain.

Over breakfast I'd almost backed out on remembering the massive roundabout on the busy A6 which I sped along five or six days a week, but it turned out that Simon had anticipated my fears and jotted down a couple of alternative routes to the lanes which he normally used, the Preston suburbs having expanded greatly since my cycling days. So it was that after wobbling along the avenue feeling like a fish out of water, or on a bike, I soon joined a B-road and then a lane which took me over the motorway and onto my old pedal-stomping ground. As you probably know, most English roads haven't been resurfaced for at least fifty years, so even the tarmac was familiar to me as I slogged along between the same old hedgerows. After stopping to lower the saddle a few millimetres my pedalling motion became more fluid and I appeared to be going much faster than I'd expected to. On crossing paths with a group of club riders I regretted my scruffy get-up, as most of them failed to return my greeting, so I resolved to wear the right gear next time.

Yes, at that point, about twenty minutes into my first real bike ride for thirty-two years, I was almost sure there'd be a next time. Once I'd settled into a comfortable cadence my fears about the traffic vanished and the damp spring air felt good as it entered my lungs. My first ride was proving far easier than my umpteenth jog, and were I to weaken I could simply change down a gear or two. Just then I felt capable of cruising right across the flatlands to Cockerham as I used to do, but I elected to err on the side of caution and follow a fairly quiet road only as far as Inskip, before wending my way back along the lanes by way of Wharles and Treales, a ride I used to easily do in an hour when I had to squeeze in a quickie between other obligations, my daily outing being sacrosanct back in the day.

After a thoroughly enjoyable half-hour or so it seemed a pity to head south so soon, but the narrow saddle was chaffing me a bit and a few spots of rain had begun to fall, so I turned left and engaged the large chainring, as I intended to motor back like a man possessed and impress Sarah – and especially Simon, who appreciated these things – by achieving an average speed of sixteen miles an hour on my first ride, and at the grand old age of sixty! Why, I surmised as I ploughed into what felt suspiciously like a headwind, at this rate within a month or so I'll be able to join Simon on his three-hour rides around the Trough of Bowland, although I may struggle a bit until I find my climbing legs.

Yes, I reflected, by June when I finally hang up my hotel keys I'll have ridden far enough and lost enough weight to keep up with that mile-eating bike collector who's never pinned on a number in his life. Oh, yes, when a former racer's muscle memory kicks in he can achieve remarkable things, I mused, before changing down two gears, as that wind was proving stronger than it felt and my arse was requested my brain for a little relief. On standing up on the pedals I discerned a distinctly spongy feeling in my thighs, so I sat down again, engaged an easier gear, and gritted my teeth. No-one said that riding sixteen miles in an hour was going to be easy, and a light rain had begun to fall, but a man who'd ridden the fifty-mile Circuit of the Dales time trial in near *blizzard* conditions could surely tough it out for a while longer and achieve his goal.

Then the road began to rise over the M55 motorway. I recalled when that essential thoroughfare had opened in the mid-seventies and how I'd charged over it as a hearty teenager, before swooping down the other side at great speed, but today the moderate rise had a wholly unforeseen effect upon my fatigued legs. On a lightweight twenty-speed bike even a casual cyclist can climb just about anything, so it came as a surprise to find that with a hundred yards to go I'd already engaged the lowest gear and was weaving slightly to lessen the gradient, a mere three or four percent, I guess. As my rotten luck would have it, just then I heard voices and turned to see a group of oldish cyclists bearing down on me, so I focussed on the tarmac beyond my front wheel and pressed the pedals with all my might.

Their voices became louder very quickly and to avoid total humiliation – in my own mind, at least – I then did something remarkably infantile for a man of my wisdom and maturity. On hearing the sound of their tyres swishing along the wet road surface I pulled over, unclipped my feet in the nick of time, dismounted, then bent over the bike, pretending to inspect the drivetrain and detect the problem which had caused a strapping chap like me to ride no faster than a toddler on a trike. All this happened very quickly and the fact that my chest was heaving like mad may have given the game away, but when one of the passing riders asked me if I was OK I managed to say, 'Yeah, jus' gears slippin', before leaning my head on the saddle and gulping in more air. One or more of them may have glanced back at me, because I heard a little chuckling as they crested the rise, so, old cycling warrior that I am, I remounted and gave chase, reasoning that once over the top my weight advantage and that muscle memory I mentioned would enable me to catch them up and tuck in behind to hide from the pesky headwind that was cramping my style.

Alas, it wasn't to be, because by the time I'd lumbered to the top they were already two hundred yards ahead, but this embarrassing encounter did have one salutary effect which I only appreciated several hours later while sipping a glass of wine. Most of the ten or so riders were at least as old as me and a few of them had distinct paunches. I felt sure that every Sunday they would ride over fifty miles, enjoy a sociable cafe stop, and arrive home feeling pleasantly tired but still able to cut the grass, wash the car, or do whatever else was required of them. Thousands of ageing men and women across the country do it every weekend and think nothing of it, and so could I… so *would* I, I swore, but that was after I'd recovered from what was about to befall me.

During those final eight miles several things happened which might well have convinced me that my three-decade break from cycling had been the best choice I'd ever made. Had I been looking for a divine message indicating that I ought to return Simon's bike right away, I could have counted them off on the fingers of a whole hand, because when the rain began to pour everything, including the rain itself, conspired to put me off cycling for the rest of my life.

Along with the unforecasted downpour came tremendous gusts of southerly wind which almost brought me to a standstill, so I immediately revised my expectations and resolved to complete my ride in an hour and a quarter. This placated me for a while and I didn't mind too much that I was getting soaked from above and below, as of course the titanium racer didn't have mudguards. On approaching the hamlet of Treales I began to divert myself by imagining I was taking part in the Tour of Flanders, that monumental Belgian classic. I was nearing the end of the 150 mile race and had just left a weakening Eddy Merckx in my wake, but Roger de Vlaeminck was clinging stubbornly to my rear wheel and I'd have to shake off the gutsy Belgian before the final excruciating climb of the Oude Kwaremont.

I think this spot of fantasising helped to increase my speed from walking to jogging pace, but the fact that I had my head down meant that I didn't see the warning signs that an old chap appeared likely to pull out in front of me. Despite my flashing front light he did, so I slammed on the brakes and shuddered to a halt about four inches from the passenger door. The myopic old duffer stopped too, then raised a bony hand and mouthed the word 'sorry', before giving me an encouraging smile and heading on his hazardous way.

"Tear up your licence!" I cried feebly, but I refrained from shaking my fist at him, as managing hotels teaches one a good deal of forbearance.

On setting off I saw that I could put the unforeseen adrenaline rush to good use and as I was now heading west the wind buffeted me from the side, so I 'sped' along, striving to hold a straight line along the rather exposed road. My line evidently wasn't straight enough for one motorist, who whizzed past within inches of my right hand, at which point my forbearance evaporated, to be replaced by blind fury, but the driver of the souped-up Fiesta was going so fast that he – surely a he – probably didn't even see my unmistakably aggressive gestures.

What with one adrenaline rush on top of another I gripped the handlebar drops and savagely pumped the pedals, but soon had to ease up, because I was approaching two female horse riders who were plodding along side by side and having a good old chinwag. As the road ahead was clear I moved right across it and passed them slowly, but still scared one of the horses, which scampered along for a few yards before the rider regained control.

"Damned cyclists," I heard one of them mutter, but by then I was past caring. I just wanted to get home, strip off my sodden togs, and have a good old think about this bike ride which had started off so well before descending into an exhausting, dangerous farce. In the event I had to dismount before then because with less than two miles to go and already back in suburbia I felt the rim of the rear wheel begin to grind against the tarmac. A puncture was the last thing I needed just then and I had a good mind to ignore it, but to ride on would have ruined the tyre and possibly damaged the expensive rim, so I regretfully rolled to a halt and propped the bike against a street sign. On the plus side the rain had ceased, but unfortunately the watery sun encouraged a couple of kids to wander down their driveway to take a look at the wet and weary crimson-faced bloke who had begun to wrestle with his rear wheel, having forgotten to engage the smallest cog before extracting it.

"Cool bike," said the twelve-year-old lad.

"Yes, it's lovely," I muttered as I pushed the wheel and pulled the rear derailleur, my hand already smeared with grease.

"Have you had a puncture?" said a younger girl, presumably his sister.

"Yes." The wheel finally fell out and might have rolled away had the lad not grabbed it. He laid it on the edge of the lawn and offered to hold the bike.

"Thanks, but I'd better put it down as I may be some time."

Happily my precious muscle memory enabled me to prise off the tyre fairly quickly and after inflating a spare inner tube slightly I shoved it in and got the tyre back on without using the levers, which raised my spirits a bit. As I was inflating it with the tiny pump the lad remarked that I didn't look like a cyclist.

I grimaced pleasantly. "That's because I'm not. I used to be and I decided to go for a ride today, but I'm afraid it's not for me any more."

The girl wrinkled her cute little nose. "You're not going to let a puncture put you off, are you?"

I straightened up and smiled sheepishly. "Well, you know, there's also the rain and bad drivers and hors... things."

The lad pointed at my soggy legs. "You need to get the right gear, then you'll like it more."

"You may be right." I swiftly inserting the wheel and shoved the old inner tube into a pocket of my cagoule, before thanking them – for their moral support, I suppose – and pushing off.

"Ride carefully!" the girl chirped, and I raised my hand, before paying heed to her advice and scrutinising every car I saw, both moving and stationary, until I reached our short cul-de-sac. I reflected that both incidents with the drivers could have been avoided if I'd paid more attention and ridden in a straighter line, but I'd have to ask Simon about how best to pass horses, because wouldn't a warning shout or the ping of a bell scare them just as much?

On spotting my Skoda saloon up ahead I put on a final spurt and in my haste to reach the garage I ended up skidding and coming to rest with a wheel under the side of Sarah's hatchback. I gazed up at the wing mirror and groaned. Surely this lamentable tumble was the final sign.

3

Simon smiled as he sipped the red wine he'd brought along on his rare Sunday evening visit. "These things happen, Tom."

"What? All that in the space of half an hour? No, I've been weighing things up this afternoon and I really think I'm going to give you the bike back. I was happy enough being a non-cyclist and all that awful ride has done is to put me in a tizzy."

"That's good."

"Is it?"

"Yes. What's happening is that the dynamic, adventurous side of your character is tussling with the indolent, cautious side. I've no doubt that while you're at work this week you'll remember the good things about the ride and you'll be raring to go again next weekend."

I sniggered. "Are you some kind of cycling psychologist, or what?"

"Well, yes, you could say that. During the thirty years I've been riding I've seen lots of folk take it up and pack it in, sometimes time and time again, and I've often asked myself why this is. I've reached the conclusion that it's perfectly understandable. In our society we're programmed to conform to a fairly rigid set of norms. We feel obliged to put work and family life above everything, so obviously an addictive and time-consuming sport like cycling is far from ideal. Those who content themselves with weekly rides in winter and a few extra outings in summer tend to stick at it, whereas those who become really hooked often find that they reach a tipping point and have to give it up, sometimes until they retire. I'm sure you're one of them."

"I'm not so sure, mate. Today's just reminded me of all the hazards of cycling that I can well do without."

He tutted and flapped his hand. "Oh, that's just the way it goes. I do twenty rides without any incidents, then one day I might come across three pillocks in an hour. On the whole drivers are considerate, but when one does annoy you it's best not to react."

"Why not?"

"Well, take that speeding driver who you threw a wobbly at. The chances are it was a young lad who'll have thought, whoops, I'd better not tangle with that big bloke who's yelling at me, but imagine the car was full of delinquents." He leant back and eyed the ceiling. "Yes, maybe one of them has just got out of prison, so to celebrate they get high on drugs and nick a car. They cut you up on purpose, then, on seeing your aggressive gestures, decide to stop and have a bit of fun. You roll to a halt and confront them, so one pulls out a knife and the others drag you into the field and beat the crap out of you. Then they leave you for dead and nick your bike, which they sell to buy more drugs."

I drained my glass. "Er, I thought you were encouraging me to take up cycling, Simon."

"I am, but the point I'm trying to make is that you never really know what type of person is behind the wheel of a vehicle. Imagine you come across a homicidal maniac in... the supermarket, for instance. You'd probably sense by their expression and body language that you oughtn't to approach that individual, but in a car you can't tell, and remember that motorised vehicles are effectively lethal weapons in the right... or rather wrong hands." He shrugged and sipped his wine. "It's just something to bear in mind."

"Oh, let's shove the bike in your car and forget about the whole thing," I whined. "Maybe I will like golf after all."

"That bike's no good to me any more."

"Why not?"

"Well, you've scratched the right pedal and torn the handlebar tape." He sighed and shook his head. "Hundred quid pedals too. No, I'm afraid you've left your indelible marks on that mile-eating machine. You've already made it your own, so you might as well get some use out of it. What's up now?"

I opened my eyes. "Your description of the assault was too vivid. I'm seeing myself lying in the field, checking for broken bones."

He laughed and topped up our glasses.

"Just tell me one thing, for future reference. How do you deal with confrontations with aggressive drivers?"

"Oh, I've had very few, but if some twerp pulls up alongside to berate or insult me I just ignore them. Only twice in all these years have I felt the need to use a little ploy that I have up my sleeve."

"What's that?"

He sprang up from the cosy chair, perched on the arm, and grasped a pair of imaginary handlebars. "Right, we're at some traffic lights and you're the aggressive driver. Now, give me a piece of your moronic mind."

I scowled at him. "Hey, you, you... flippin' pest."

He flicked his brake lever and looked calmly ahead.

"I'm talking to you, you... damned cyclist!"

He prodded his imaginary cycle computer.

I growled. "When we set off I'm gonna run you off the road, you... infernal nuisance!"

"You're a terrible actor," he murmured. "But here goes." He turned his head slowly to face me and without a flicker of emotion said the following. "I've got your registration number and my colleagues will be in touch." He eyed the road ahead once more.

"Is that it?"

He smiled. "It worked both times."

"But isn't that sort of impersonating a policeman or something?"

He shrugged. "I might have meant a gaggle of dentists with sharpened scalpels, but it did the trick." He slithered back onto the cushion. "The thing to remember is this. Most drivers are sensible, rational beings, but a tiny proportion of them are morons. You'd ignore a moron in a shop or a pub or wherever, so you must also ignore them on the road. We can't allow them or the mere thought of them to stop us doing what we enjoy. If we did that, football crowds would fall by ninety-five percent overnight. Anyway, enough about that boring stuff. So, what was your average speed when you reached Inskip?"

I smiled. "16.2 miles an hour. I really thought I was flying, but it was just the massive tailwind pushing me along."

"Hmm, but it's still pretty good for a first outing."

I sighed. "It was 11.3 by the time I reached home."

"Not bad, considering all those incidents."

"The clock stops when you stop, as you know."

He twiddled his glass and examined the contents. "Take it off."

"What?"

"The computer. You didn't have one back in the day and it's the last thing you need right now. When do you retire exactly?"

"I've just six weeks left."

"Put it back on when you finish, if you must. I never pay any attention to my average speed, though I must say I do like to see my mileage."

"Oh, I don't know, Simon. I'm truly grateful for the offer of the bike, but... like you said, it's put me in a tizzy."

"Don't be soft, Tom. Go out once a week if you feel like it, then when you're a free man you can decide if you want to do more."

"Hmm. Wou... would you like to come out with me next weekend?"

"Nope."

"Oh, right. Yes, I suppose I'd slow you down too much."

"It's not that. I don't care how fast I go. My speed, if you must know, averages between about fourteen and seventeen miles an hour, the latter when I ride on the flat with my fitter friends. If you need me to spur you on I'll come for a ride, but knowing your character you're better off going it alone at first."

"Any particular reason?"

"Because you're a born competitor. That's how you became such a hotshot in hotel management."

I shrugged modestly. "A decent hotel fixer, I suppose, but I never wanted to go down south or abroad. Ah, you know, I always fancied managing the original Raffles Hotel in Singapore, but I doubt I'd have achieved that, however hard I'd tried."

"It wouldn't have been how you'd imagined it anyway. Yes, if I were you I'd ride solo for now and get stronger little by little, without comparing yourself to anyone else. I think cycling's a personal thing and better appreciated alone, although it's nice to go out with others too."

I leant back and closed my eyes. "It did feel good to be whizzing along for a while with the wind in my... helmet."

"Yes, and I think pedalling has a kind of mesmeric effect. Do you know what Émile Zola said about cycling?"

"The novelist? Did they have bikes in his day?"

"Yes, when he was exiled in London at the end of the nineteenth century he cycled a lot. In fact he carried a camera on his bike, because he enjoyed taking photos of other cyclists, especially ladies. Anyway, he said something like, 'I love the bicycle for the oblivion it gives. No matter how much I walk, I think. On my bicycle I go in the wind, I no longer think, and nothing is so delicious as rest.' I couldn't agree with him more. On the bike I haven't got a care in the world, whereas walking or just sitting I'm apt to remember troublesome bridges or tricky extractions, not to mention other worldly cares."

"Today, while the going was good, I only thought about the ride and how fast I was going."

"Take the computer off."

"Is he back on track?" Sarah said from the doorway.

"Yes, I'm sure he'll be out for another little ride next weekend. Have some wine."

At the hotel on Monday morning a strange feeling came over me and after regretfully informing the accountant that I had to cancel our game of golf due to family commitments I summoned the assistant manager to my office. Andy was an ambitious Lancaster lad of thirty-two who was dead-set on replacing me as manager once I left. This wouldn't be easy, because the hotel belongs to a chain and he'd have to overcome some serious competition, especially from colleagues in the south who were dying to relocate and finally be able to afford a decent house. Some of these people would have more experience and superior qualifications to Andy, so I told him not to get his hopes up too much.

He nodded. "I know, Tom, but I'm still hopeful." He grinned. "You'll put a good word in for me, won't you?"

"I'm going to recommend you as my successor and even try to pull a few strings, because I know you can do the job, but…" I gazed out of the third-floor window at the sliver of

Morecambe Bay I could see. "But the big shots might argue that you lack experience. They'll want someone who can hit the ground running and I've had an idea which might improve your chances."

"What's that? I'll do whatever it takes."

I clasped my skull and pressed it softly. "Oh, I feel a migraine coming on."

He stood up. "I'll get you some paracetamol."

"No, it won't happen until tomor... no, forget that idea, as I'm a lousy actor. No, er... have I ever mentioned my Aunt... Ivy to you?"

"No."

"Well, she's my late mother's sister and she's very poorly. She didn't have children, so I'm having to visit her quite often. In the care home they say she hasn't got long to live, so tomorrow I'm going to have to leave at midday to go to see her. The way things are going I think I'll have to do that about twice a week from now on, probably on Tuesdays and Thursdays, so you'll be in charge and I'll make sure you have plenty to do. That way when I come to pull strings I'll be able to say that you're well capable of running the place. How does that sound?"

He smiled. "Unconvincing, Tom. With so few weeks left I guess you can do what the hell you like from now on. Some would just go on the sick, but you'll not want to give the wrong impression after all you've done here."

"Oh, forget about me. Think about yourself. That's the only way to get ahead in this game."

"All right, but I'm afraid we're going to have to hospitalise your aunt."

"Oh, dear. Why's that?"

"I believe you can visit care homes in the evenings, but if hospital visiting time is… two to three, say, you'll have to leave here at midday."

I slapped my desk. "Brilliant! You'll make a great manager."

"And that way you could nip off most days if you wanted to."

"Hmm…" My legs still felt fatigued after the previous day's ride. "No, that would be overkill. In fact… yes, this week I'll only visit her on Wednesday, then as she weakens I'll go more often and you'll have more stuff to do."

He sniggered. "That suits me, but what's this all about?"

"Oh, you know, just a bit of laziness creeping in right at the end."

"I don't believe that. I even think you'll be sad to go in a way."

I stood up and walked to the window, before tensing my tummy muscles and walking back. "I've taken up cycling again."

"Oh, right."

"Are you not surprised? At my age, I mean?"

"Course not. Everyone's at it these days. Personally I find cyclists a bit of a pest, especially on a Sunday when I want to give the car some welly for once."

I growled inwardly, but let it pass. "I used to ride a lot, you see, but now I'm so unfit that I think the thing to do is to get out little and often. Right, let's have a think about what you can do in my absence."

"Tell me a bit more about Aunt Ivy first, so we'll get our stories straight. You don't want to miss out on any golden handshakes they might have in mind."

"Fat chance of that, but Aunt Ivy... well, she's eighty-nine, so she's had a good innings, but I think she's just going to fade away during the coming weeks, but not quite die, as I don't want to be playing the bereaved nephew. So, on Wednesday, after double-checking the bookings, you'll take a turn around the kitchens, before having a word with the housekeeper about absentees, then...

So it was that on Wednesday afternoon I went for my second ride, along the exact same route, as I wished to exorcise Sunday's demons. This I managed to achieve, because although overcast it didn't rain, no drivers endangered me, I didn't puncture and, most gratifying of all, I conquered the major climb – the motorway bridge – in *second* gear, although my lungs were fit to burst on cresting the rise. When fit people take up cycling it's mainly their leg muscles which have to adapt and they don't often get out of breath until their expanding thighs and calves begin to demand a faster flow of blood – no scientific jargon here – but as I hadn't jogged at all for over three months I knew that my lung capacity and muscular strength ought to improve at the same slow rate, as I had no illusions about becoming a speed merchant overnight, if ever, because I wasn't convinced that this muscle memory business would really benefit me. Some studies say that it lasts for up to fifteen years, while other experts believe it may be a lifelong phenomenon, up to a point, so I decided to side with these optimistic bods and hope for the best.

Then again, I asked myself later as I relaxed on the sofa, sipping a smoothie, did it really matter how strong I became, as long as I could propel myself along at a reasonable rate of knots? I'd paid heed to Simon and removed the cycle computer, but of course I knew the distance and my watch enabled me to roughly calculate my average speed – a little under thirteen miles an hour. I realised there and then that wherever I rode I'd inevitably determine the distance on Google Maps and also have a good idea as to how long it had taken me, so, bowing to the inevitable, I put the computer back on, though I swore not to look at it until the end of each ride.

Fat chance of that, I said to myself on Saturday morning as I hammered along the road between Inskip and Broughton, determined to achieve an average speed of 14mph on my twenty-mile ride. I had a few tenths in hand and was loath to turn onto a quieter lane which would have slowed me down, so I ended up on the A6 and had to negotiate that extremely busy roundabout before stopping the clock on entering our estate, as my average was in grave danger of dropping to 13.9, which would have been a tragedy after all the effort I'd put it.

I strode proudly into the kitchen and told Sarah of my marvellous accomplishment.

She glanced up from the musical score she was perusing. "That's nice. Take those shoes off in here."

I complied before giving her a blow-by-blow account of my ride.

"The A6? And that huge roundabout? I can't remember seeing cyclists on it."

I scratched my sweaty head. "Yes, well, there is a sort of cycle path, but it would have slowed me down too much, and I really wanted to do 14mph."

"Why?"

"Er, well, it's a nice round number, and thirteen's unlucky, isn't it?"

"I see, so after all your moaning about the traffic that's stopped you cycling for thirty years, you risk life and limb with all those speeding cars so that one number rather than another appears on the screen."

I eyed her sulkily. "Well I think I did quite well, all things considered."

"And I think you need your head examining." She closed her eyes and inhaled deeply through her nostrils. "Oh, yes, this is taking me back to the days before we got married. You'd rattle on about your times and speed and sprockets and God knows what else. I thought I was going out with some kind of mad cycling scientist."

I sighed. "You went on about your music too."

"Until I realised that you didn't listen to a word I said. You still wouldn't know a pizzicato if it slapped you in the face."

"Plucking," I muttered. "Now, what's your gripe, exactly?"

"I fear that you're beginning where you left off. I assumed that you'd treat cycling as a pleasant pastime that would get you out and about and keep you fit, but you're already pushing yourself and taking stupid risks on the roads."

"I won't go that way again," I mumbled.

"Fetch me that computer thing."

"What for?"

She smiled. "I don't really believe you did fourteen miles an hour. It sounds awfully fast."

"Ha!" In a jiffy I was back with the slim device. "Here, you see, and look, the distance, and here's my total so far, almost fifty-five miles."

She took it and wandered over to the sink, where she pressed the buttons and appeared to be ruminating on my stats.

"And when I buy a chest strap it'll tell me my heart rate too."

She groaned and dropped it into a panful of water. I sprang to my feet to retrieve it, but she held me off with a spatula.

"Stay back! This is for your own good."

"Lemme get it!"

"Can't you see it's for the best, you numpty?"

I deftly wrong-footed her and managed to scoop it out, but after a few frantic blinks it expired in my hand. "You silly... moo cow. Simon won't be impressed, you know. Are you going to attack the bike with an axe too?"

She slapped my cheeks lightly. "Bike good, computer bad."

"Bah!"

"Cycling good, obsession with speed foolish and counterproductive."

"Pah!"

"And even dangerous, as we've seen today."

"But now I won't even know how far I've been."

"If it's too difficult for you, I'll personally measure your route afterwards."

On remembering those handy online maps I cheered up a bit. In the old days I'd had to physically measure the miles on an Ordinance Survey map, sometimes cheating a bit, but now it could be done accurately in a few moments. I gave the defunct device one last shake, before chucking it in the bin. On recalling my hazardous circumnavigation of the scary roundabout and my total absence of fear I knew she was right, in all respects. I'd got off on the wrong foot and would have to reassess my reasons for getting back on my bike.

4

During the following weeks I often pictured the cycle computer in the sink and felt truly grateful that Sarah had performed her act of constructive destruction, because once liberated from my obsession with average speed – which would only have worsened, I knew – I was able to enjoy my rides far more. I still powered along occasionally and always attacked that motorway bridge as if the world champion's rainbow jersey would be presented to me at the top, but most of the time I just pedalled serenely along, gazing across the flat fields and thinking about nothing in particular.

After citing Aunt Ivy's illness that first time I decided to make her well again and thenceforth told my staff that I was taking Wednesday afternoons off to go cycling. I'd put in hundreds of extra hours in my quest to restore the hotel's fortunes, so even my boss in London didn't blink an eye during our occasional video calls. I still gave Andy plenty of extra responsibilities and backed him to the hilt, but unfortunately he didn't get my job in the end, so a few weeks later he jumped ship and went to manage the hotel of a rival chain in Windermere.

It was great to be back on the bike just for the fun of it and after thrice-weekly rides for about a month I felt ready to head for the hills. To do this I rode east from Fulwood to the hamlet of Haighton Green, after which I took a narrow lane north to avoid the town of Longridge and steered a serpentine course toward the towering Beacon Fell. This wooded hill which rises above the undulating countryside reminded me of the Puy de Dôme in central France, scene of many epic Tour de France battles. The fact that the Puy is an extinct volcano rising almost five thousand feet above sea level while Beacon Fell measures a measly 873 feet is unimportant, because for me at this early stage of my cycling comeback it was a formidable challenge.

Having thus far only tested my climbing legs on the motorway bridge and a somewhat harder drag into the small town of Kirkham, I was ill prepared for the harsh gradients of the lanes on the fringes of the Forest of Bowland, so on my first Beacon Fell outing I just rode around it and psyched myself up for an attempt on the summit at a later date. A mere glimpse of the steep lane to the top told me that my largest 28-tooth sprocket might not be big enough to prevent me from grinding to a halt and having to push the bike, which brings me onto the subject of gear – as in equipment – a theme dear to the hearts of all but a few hardy cyclists who ride the same bike for decades and ignore every new innovation.

If you read about cycling online you'll see that gear rears its tempting head on almost every web page, with seductive links to products you didn't know you needed or didn't even realise existed until that moment. Should you also watch a few of the plethora of YouTube cycling videos, you'll soon discover that every item you possess, from your helmet down to your shoe cleats, are inferior, outdated products which will make you the laughing stock of every self-respecting modern-day cyclist.

As I was lucky enough to be the owner of an excellent and only slightly outdated road bike, the sole purchases I made for it were some special clip-on mudguards for bikes without brazed on eyelets, a fresh pair of tyres to put on the moment I'd worn mine out, a spare chain, spare brake blocks, spare cables, special bike oil, degreaser, some dinky rechargeable lights to avoid accumulating piles of used lithium batteries, and a few more bits and bobs. Modern road bikes have eleven or even twelve sprockets on the rear wheel, but I was more than happy with the ten which mine possessed, until I saw the lane up to Beacon Fell, that is. I decided to consult my cycling guru about this weighty matter.

Simon laughed down the phone. "You used to have to climb hills like that on a 42×23 gear, unless you had a touring bike like me."

"Yes, but that was then and this is now."

"34×28 should get you up just about anything if you take your time, so don't fret about it."

"Can't I get a cassette with a 32 sprocket, at least?"

"You can, but you'll also need a new rear derailleur and a longer chain. That'll set you back at least a couple of hundred quid, unless you want to sully the bike with inferior components."

"And if, er... I wanted to go eleven speed?"

"Ah, well, then you'd also need a new chainset and new levers. If you get the right ones, that extra sprocket will end up costing you… oh, I think a grand should cover it, if you shop around."

I gasped. "A *grand*?"

"Yes, for the right stuff. It'd be a lot cheaper to incorporate more climbing into your rides and lose some weight."

"I've already lost close to half a stone. I'm down to thirteen-six, in the morning after having a pee and before drinking anything."

He chuckled. "And when you were racing?"

"Oh, well, I weighed about eleven and a half, but I was much younger then."

"So?"

"Well, I've filled out, haven't I?"

"Since you were twenty-seven? In what way?"

"Well, you just do, don't you?"

"Have your shoulders widened and your ribcage expanded?"

I prodded my chest. "Er, I don't think so."

"Well then? I haven't gained an ounce in the last thirty years."

I pulled a face at the phone. "Lucky you."

"There's no need to be too extreme, but you're certainly carrying a stone of excess fat."

I grasped my slightly slimmer midriff. "But where is it? I mean, fourteen pounds is a hell of a lot. Imagine buying that much meat and hanging it on your body."

He laughed. "You're covered in fat from head to foot, or from neck to ankle. Not that much of it, but it's there all right, spread all over you. I hope you don't quaff a litre of coke or something after your rides, or stuff yourself full of cakes."

I pictured the huge lump of buttered Parkin I'd devoured the previous day, washed down by a pint or so of extremely sweet tea. "Er, no, I don't touch soft drinks."

"Forget about that extra sprocket, Tom. Instead remember that you're effectively carrying the equivalent of a pannier full of stuff right now. Shed that stone and you'll fly up the hills like Bahamontes," he said, referring to the great Spanish climber who won the 1959 Tour de France and is still looking fit in his nineties.

In view of what the future was to bring, Simon's pannier analogy seems somehow prophetic, but I mustn't get ahead of myself.

Anyway, as I intended to slim down I felt that I'd saved myself a grand, so I got the go-ahead from Sarah to expand my cycling wardrobe. Nowadays many cyclists tend to favour dull colours, especially if they buy their clothing from trendy brands like Rapha, whereas others prefer to sport fluorescent garments from head to foot. The former contingent rarely use lights, which would cramp their style, whereas the latter prefer extremely bright ones, especially the headlamps, which dazzle every living being that crosses their path. I think these riding lighthouses are guilty of overkill, while the cool dudes are putting themselves in unnecessary danger, especially on overcast days, so I decided to steer a middle course and buy light-coloured tops, complemented by fluorescent track mitts, socks and some cute little lycra toe covers for summer use. This way the motorists would see bright bits moving about, but wouldn't suffer from scorched retinas as they passed me by. On a more serious note, I discovered that flashing lights can cause epilepsy sufferers to have seizures, so I began to leave my lights on a constant beam instead. Enough boring gear talk, for now.

By the time I retired two weeks later I'd conquered Beacon Fell three times and enjoyed riding around the leafy one-way lane which circumnavigates the summit, before plunging down the other side and making my way home. One sunny Sunday I crossed paths with lots of other cyclists on those quiet roads and at least a dozen whizzed past me, though I did pass a few, usually mounted on mountain or touring bikes and enjoying the scenery even more than me, as I often forgot to look around when I was grinding up yet another slope.

"You've yet to sample the social side of cycling, by the sound of it," Simon said during the dinner to celebrate my retirement which Sue had cooked for us. "Do you never talk to other cyclists?"

"Oh, I say the odd word when they pass me or I pass them, but I'm out of breath half the time."

He tutted. "You're still trying too hard then. Now that you're going to have all the time in the world to ride, I think you ought to slow down and begin to communicate with your fellow riders."

"Yes, well, I wouldn't mind that, but the fast guys won't want to stop to chat to a slowcoach like me, and... this risotto is delicious, Sue."

"Thanks."

"You were about to say?" said Simon.

"Oh, I've sometimes passed old guys who look like real stalwarts and could probably tell me a tale or two, but... well, I'm loath to break my rhythm, so I tend to push on."

He sighed. "I think it's about time you came out with me then."

Already flushed by the food and wine, my face coloured even more. "Wow, did you hear that, Sarah? Simon's finally deigned to go for a ride with me! What an honour, after making excuses for weeks."

"I wanted you to find your feet alone. Besides, the friends I go out with would have been too fast and might have demoralised you, but I think you'll be fit enough to keep up now."

"Yes... oh, I sometimes miss the cycle computer that Sarah so wantonly destroyed. I reckon I'm averaging 15mph on the flat now, but I can't be sure."

"It doesn't matter," said Simon. "Anyway, if you come out with us tomorrow I can give you the data at the end of the ride."

"Really? Can I come?"

"Yes, if you feel up to it. We're just going around the Trough of Bowland, as Frank has to be home early."

I gulped. "Just the Trough, yes." I pushed away my wine glass and pictured that steep ribbon of road which cuts through the Forest of Bowland. If Beacon Fell was my Puy de Dôme, the Trough was something akin to my Mont Ventoux, that singular six-thousand-foot mountain in Provence where Tom Simpson collapsed and died in the 1967 Tour de France. Although I didn't expect to meet the same fate as that cycling hero whose desire for success was just too great, it would test me to the limit, unless... "Which, er... way are we going up the Trough?"

He grinned. "From Dunsop Bridge, of course."

I cringed. "Ah, yes, good."

"It's the best way, as you get such a lovely long downhill alongside the river. When I climb something hard I like to get my reward. More wine?"

"No, I'd better not."

He chuckled and half-filled my glass. "Don't worry, Tom, it's just a social run, like all my rides."

"He won't sleep for fretting about it now," said Sarah.

"How far is it?" I asked Simon.

"About forty-five miles the way we go."

I frowned. "The furthest I've ridden so far is thirty-six."

He patted me on the back. "You'll be fine."

Four of us met up not far from Fulwood the following sunny morning at nine and on seeing Simon's mates I felt mightily relieved. Next to the lithe dentist on his super-light racing machine they looked far more pedestrian on their more modest bikes and with just as much fatty padding as me. Frank was a sixty-one-year-old plumber from Penwortham, to the south of Preston, who Simon had met on a ride about fifteen years ago. They'd hit it off so well, partly due to their shared love of cycling history, that they'd arranged to meet up again and soon become great riding buddies. Simon had told the other chap, Mark, about his hobby while clamping one of his molars a few years earlier and it turned out that the now fifty-nine-year-old car mechanic was on the comeback trail after many cycling-free years due to family commitments. Mark had gelled with the others – for Simon's posse usually numbered between four and eight riders – and joined the group.

Two more regulars hadn't been able to make it that day, so the four of us were soon trundling eastwards at what seemed to me like a very easy pace indeed.

"Bit slow this," I murmured to Simon as we followed the wheels of the other two.

"Our old muscles need time to warm up," he said, before slipping behind me as a car approached, despite the road being wide enough for it to pass. I soon noticed that while we usually rode two-abreast when the coast was clear, whenever a vehicle was heard behind us we always singled out, and on the busier road to Longridge no attempt was made to pair up at all. When we crossed paths with a dozen-strong group of club riders all riding two-abreast I snuck up to Simon's shoulder and asked him why we weren't doing likewise.

"We've as much right to be on the road as the cars, after all, and on a Sunday no-one ought to be hurrying," I added.

"Well, in a larger group it can be safer to ride like that, as when drivers see a long line of cyclists they sometimes assume it's all right to pass when it might not be. Groups like that ought to single out from time to time, but some clubs are reluctant to do so. As you know, I rode with the Preston Wheelers for a while, many years ago, but when long queues of cars began to build up behind us it made me nervous, because who was to say that one of the drivers wasn't a loony who might lose his patience and just go for it round a bend?" He glanced over his shoulder. "Drop back, Tom."

After we'd cautiously traversed Longridge, Simon went on to say that an important characteristic of his group was their fluid riding formation which enabled them to seamlessly single out and double up without uttering a word. "It's how we like it and we rarely have issues with drivers. When they're especially considerate we always thank them with a wave, so at least we're doing our bit for harmonious road use, unlike plenty of others. How are you doing?"

I pointed at Frank and Mark who were chatting away in front of us. "This is a bit on the slow side, to be honest."

He smiled. "Don't forget the Trough."

Piece of cake at this rate, I thought.

"And Oakenclough on the way back."

"Ah," I said, remembering the roller-coaster nature of that particular route. "Why not Scorton and the flat roads back?"

"We like our hills, as you'll see."

"Right."

At this point I must remember Sarah's warning not to go into unnecessary and mind-numbing detail about each of my cycling battles. It's all right for me to give her lengthy post-ride debriefings, she says, because it usually goes in one ear and out of the other, but to subject my readers to such tedious narratives will be a sure way of losing them before my story's really got going. Sound advice, no doubt, so I'll try to keep this one short and sweet, rather like the Trough of Bowland climb, or the hard bit, because the road rises gradually alongside the river for a while before it veers off and tilts upwards for an excruciating mile with sections of over fifteen percent, though that day they felt more like fifty.

As we rode along the lovely flat stretch of road between Whitewell and Dunsop Bridge I felt sure I was going to give a good account of myself up the Trough. Our pace had been easy-peasy and I rather fancied unleashing the so-far underexploited power of my now quite lean and muscly legs. It wouldn't do to forge ahead, of course, as I was a guest and as such ought to respect the etiquette of the group, so when we turned left onto the narrower road to the summit I really hoped that one of the guys would put on a spurt and shake things up a bit. I guessed that Simon, the lightest by far and on a fifteen-pound bike, would gradually distance the others, in which case I'd bide my time for a while and lull them into a false sense of security, before passing them and trying to bridge the gap across to my friend. He might be so surprised, I surmised as we tackled the early slopes at a comfortable pace, that if I had the strength I'd ride straight past and attempt to reach the summit alone, like a slightly oversized Marco Pantani in his frequent Alpine battles with Miguel Indurain. There I'd politely wait for them, before modestly admitting that the few hundred miles I'd done so far appeared to have gone some way to reactivating my racing legs, because of course none of them had competed on the bike in their lives, unlike me.

On a short, sharp rise before the climb proper my muscle memory must have recalled those bygone days, because I found myself out of the saddle and forging to the top, before coasting down past a butty van with the three of them trailing in my wake. As I'd been a little naughty I considered compounding my transgression and pressing on to the top, before apologising for my impulsive behaviour and promising not to do it again, cross my cranks and hope to die.

I needn't have worried, because no sooner had I begun to pedal again than Mark hurtled past pushing a surprisingly big gear, closely followed by Frank, who was twiddling away like Chris Froome en route to demoralising his opponents once more. I gritted my teeth and dug deep, expecting Simon to dance past on his featherweight climbing machine, but he remained close behind me, so all was not lost after all. Although amazed that those two fairly hefty guys could climb so fast, it was Simon I really wanted to match up the Trough – or even beat, I confess – so I dug in and found myself able to remain just twenty yards behind the oddly matched pair. The fact that we'd yet to reach the really steep bit had slipped my mind and I had an inkling that I was already breathing far too hard. Still, Simon was behind me, so he was probably suffering too, I thought, until he pulled up alongside, pedalling smoothly.

"I'd slow down a bit, if I were you, Tom, because that ramp up ahead is a real killer," he said calmly.

"Hmm," I said on exhaling.

He laughed. "Those two always set off too fast, but on a hill like this you've got to pace yourself."

I just nodded and stood up on the pedals.

"If I were you I'd change down to bottom… oh, you're already in it. Oh, well, it's early days yet," he said just as we hit the ramp.

Later I would complain to Sarah that he'd mercilessly attacked me on the climb, but in reality he'd just continued at the same cadence while I'd almost ground to a halt on the hideously steep strip of tarmac. Almost, but not quite, because by means of an almost superhuman effort I managed to keep the pedals turning *just* fast enough to avoid falling off. When the gradient eased a fraction I looked up to see Simon, still seated, sailing past his mates, who appeared to be flailing about almost as desperately as me. The rest of the ascent was a veritable war of attrition between me and gravity and my sole ambition was to avoid the humiliation – in my own mind, at least – of placing a foot on the ground, which would have forced me to dismount and ignominiously push my bike to the top.

Funnily enough it was during this period of intense self-torture when I wondered for the first time if I ought to have asked my doctor to give me the once-over before submitting my unaccustomed body to such extreme trials, because Beacon Fell had been tough too, but nothing like this. I actually managed to grin on reflecting that my heart had to be in good shape to lug my carcass this far up the hill without exploding and I was still grinning when I reached the top and wobbled to a halt alongside the others.

"Well done, Tom!" Simon cried, before giving me a hearty slap on the back. "I thought you might have to get off and push."

"Never," I wheezed, before communing with my handlebars until my breathing had slowed somewhat. "Set off too fast though. Soon get fitter… ride up sitting down… like you."

"Only a mountain goat like Simon can do that," said a flushed Frank. "The Trough's never easy for us heavyweights."

"I beat him this time," Mark said to Simon.

"You shoved me into the side," Frank protested.

"Bollocks."

"Broke my stride. I'll have you on the next hill."

"Yeah, right. Get moving, you moaning git."

After this bout of light-hearted bickering we began to coast down the other side and when the gradient eased alongside the river an atmosphere of juvenile jollity persisted as the two men ribbed each other and Simon vividly described my face as I'd battled up the last few yards of the climb, bobbing from side to side like the pre-war Tour de France heroes who had to push tremendously hard gears up the Pyrenean and Alpine passes. I think we were all a bit euphoric and while these days this sensation is explained by endorphins and whatnot, I only know that I felt tremendously alive as we freewheeled along like a group of giddy teenagers. During my recent solo rides I'd had many spells of serene satisfaction and the occasional moment of elation, but alongside that crystalline stream I realised that even more fun was to be had when riding with others. Realised rather than remembered, because during my last few cycling years in my twenties I'd almost always ridden alone, having had insufficient spare time to bother with Sunday club rides and suchlike.

"This takes me back to my teens," I said to Simon. "When me and a couple of mates used to shoot off for a week or a weekend, staying at youth hostels or even camping."

"Until the racing bug bit you, yes. When I retire I'd like to do some touring." He applied the brakes. "Left here, and prepare for another climb."

"Oh, goody."

Between Marshaw and Scorton the narrow road follows a burbling brook before rising steadily between fields and moorland. After a sharp dip and a cattle grid, Mark and Frank resumed their climbing battle – reminiscent of those between the two post-war Italian aces, Coppi and Bartali, Simon remarked – while he rode alongside me, setting a pace which he judged I could maintain to the top. After meeting our gasping companions and descending to a crossroads he offered to accompany me down to Scorton and onto the easy roads home.

"If you feel you've done enough climbing for one day."

I looked ahead at the Fylde flatlands, then left at the rising hillside. "No, I'm up for Oakenclough, I think."

"Good man. Just let me put these two in their place, then I'll keep you company on the other hills."

The initial Oakenclough climb is the hardest and I maintained a slow enough pace to enable me to enjoy watching Simon toy with the other two for a while, before rising from the saddle for the first time that day and accelerating away at a remarkable speed for a man of fifty-eight, no matter how light he and his bike might be. Over the top we stopped to admire the view of Morecambe Bay beyond Heysham's incongruous nuclear power station and I asked Simon if he'd ever considered doing veterans' road races.

"Not really."

"In the hilly races I'm sure you'd do really well, and just think, two years from now you'll be a spring chicken in the over-sixties category. Then you'd really kick some ass, as the saying goes."

He wiped a single bead of sweat from his left temple. "Yes, well, I know from Strava that I climb pretty well for my age, but competing is really the last thing I want to do. When I retire I want freedom, not obligations, however self-imposed they might be."

"I see. What's Strava?"

"It's bloody great," said Mark.

Simon sighed. "It's something I shouldn't have mentioned to you."

"But what is it?"

"It's this thing where you can track your–"

"Shush, Frank," said Simon. "Sorry, but you can't break Strava to a man like Tom just like that. He'll need some counselling first, as it can be a dangerous thing in the wrong hands."

"Is it a drug?" I said.

"In a manner of speaking, yes. Come on, let's get you over these last hills."

I was in no state to quiz Simon as I crawled up two more nasty little slopes, and once on the familiar flat roads beyond Garstang my fatigue was such that I couldn't spare the energy to speak. At Catforth we said goodbye to Frank and Mark, who were hurrying home, before Simon led me along a narrow lane to Roots Cafe, an establishment adjoining a cluster of craft studios which had recently become very popular with cyclists from miles around.

"I prefer a cafe stop near the end of my rides," Simon said as we grabbed the last free table outside, as the place was heaving with riders from all over Lancashire and Merseyside, plus a few civilians too. The sun was warm and nobody appeared to be hurrying to get back on the road.

I gazed around approvingly. "You know, I hardly ever went to cafes during my last years of riding. Never had the time."

"Well, this is just the place to tell you about Strava and issue my personal health warning about it."

"I'm intrigued."

"Let's order some food."

Over our succulent bacon and sausage butties Simon explained that Strava is a website which enables one to track all kinds of sporting activities, from alpine skiing to kayaking, and which is especially popular with cyclists and runners.

"Right, that sounds fine, but why might it endanger my health?"

He smiled. "I mean your mental health, mainly, although folk have died because of it."

"How?"

"Well, the potentially dangerous aspect of Strava are the segments. Riders can establish them along stretches of road wherever they want, then everyone can compare their times over them. The most hotly contested segments are on climbs, but nowadays they're everywhere, including downhills, although those are sometimes removed because folk have been badly injured or even killed while flying down them at breakneck speed, literally. The flat segments have their dangers too. A pair of American cyclists were filmed riding in a hurricane, a real hurricane, trying to beat some Strava time or other."

"How crazy. That sort of thing wouldn't tempt me, as I'm a steady descender and I never go out in hurricanes. So, how do you get–"

"The danger of Strava to you," he interrupted. "Is that once you found out where the segments were you'd probably try to beat your previous times on every ride. You'd try to beat my times too, and those of anyone else you know, until every outing would become like a race."

"I see. Does your use of the conditional tense mean that you strongly disapprove of me joining the ranks of those who must surely get a lot of enjoyment out of it, including yourself?"

He shrugged. "I just like to see my route and my distance, but do as you wish. I'm merely pointing out the pitfalls of it for a man of your temperament. I know it had a very adverse effect on one member of our group."

"How was that?"

He smiled. "He got hooked. You can pay for more advanced features and he became obsessed by being at the top of his age group ranking. He'd just retired, you see, so he had plenty of time to train. He soon stopped coming out with us, because when we rolled slowly through his precious segments he got withdrawal symptoms, especially if there was a tailwind, obviously the best time to make an attempt." He topped up our mugs from the teapot. "He used to study the wind direction every morning then plan his routes accordingly, often driving somewhere first to tackle new segments. One windy morning he drove to Derbyshire to ride the Cat and Fiddle pass. He only achieved the fifth best time in his age group, so he drove down again the following week."

"Ha, he must have been keen."

"Yes, and the last I heard he'd sold the aerodynamic bike he'd bought expressly to improve his Strava times and gone back to work."

"What?"

"He's a builder and folk were pestering him to do jobs, so I believe he took on a big project to avoid having to go out on the bike and ride himself into the ground every day."

"I wouldn't be like that."

"Hmm, I'm not so sure. All your routes are chock-a-block with segments, you know. Besides, haven't you enjoyed your cycling more since Sarah drowned your computer?"

"Your computer, yes. Well, I'll do without it for now then. Oh, and why is this a good place to tell me about the dreaded Strava?"

He smiled. "Look around you. Cyclists from all over the place, sharing tables and chatting away with folk they've never set eyes on before. This cafe's becoming a real cyclists' hub and you ought to drop in on your way home sometimes. During the week I bet you'll see the same faces and meet some interesting people, and you'll be in no hurry to get home now, you lucky sod."

I nodded. "It hasn't quite sunk in yet that I've retired."

"It will tomorrow morning, and every other weekday from now on. Here you might meet people to ride with too."

"Yes, I'd like that. I've enjoyed it today and I'd like to come out with you again."

"You'll be welcome."

I grinned. "So have I made the grade?"

"You're well on the way to making it, and whenever blokes retire they seem to grow wings within a few weeks. More riding and more rest do wonders for one's fitness."

I pictured myself flying up the Trough of Bowland, aided by a nifty pair of carbon wings. "I can't wait to start my new life. It'll feel like... like a kind of rebirth."

He smiled. "Yes, and as in every life, the formative years are the crucial ones. There's an awful lot of enjoyment to be had out of cycling, if you approach it in the right way."

"Heavy-handed hint taken, Simon. Come on, let's get going before rigor mortis sets into my knackered legs."

5

It was at about this time that cycling began to crop up more often in my dreams. Even during my long years of exile from the sport I'd occasionally dreamt I was riding my bike, but now cycling-themed dreams began to haunt my every sleeping hour. That night, for some reason, I dreamt I was riding along the seafront at Blackpool with huge waves bursting against the sea walls and soaking me through. I awoke at ten to seven, my usual time, to find Sarah creeping around the still darkened room.

I yawned. "No need to be quiet, love. I'll be getting up at seven, as always."

"I thought you might like a lie-in on your first day of freedom."

"Nope, I shan't be heading down that slippery slope to lazi... sloth." I threw back the lightweight duvet. "I'm raring to go."

She opened the curtains. "It's raining."

"What?" I rushed to the window and gazed down at the sodden back garden. "I didn't expect this."

"No, we've had such a good run of fine weather that I didn't look at the forecast either. Oh, well. What will you do today?"

"I was going to... I *am* going to go cycling. Can't let a few drops of rain stop me."

"Rather you than me. Why don't you rest and do those little jobs you said you'd do?"

"There'll be time enough for that too."

After breakfast I waved her off from the doorstep, before entering the garage and affixing the clip-on mudguards I'd yet to put through their paces, as they'd only had a dry run to make sure they didn't scrape or wobble. As the rain pattered on the metal door I told myself I ought to have a rest day and do something else, but I'd been so looking forward to my first retirement ride that I simply had to get out, if only for an hour or so. Then I smiled on remembering the cafe. It was about six miles from home, so I could approach it via a roundabout route, have a chinwag with the other hardy pedallers who'd also braved the rain, then fly straight home and jump in the shower. After that I'd set about changing a couple of tap washers, painting that stained corner of the spare bedroom, hoovering the whole house, cleaning the crumb-infested toaster, and generally impressing my wife with my dynamic retirement debut.

As the rain hadn't eased by ten I reluctantly wheeled out my bike and by the time I reached the lanes my legs were as soaked as on that testing maiden ride, but lycra and bare skin handle water better than baggy trackie bottoms and my super-duper new rain jacket appeared to be doing its job of keeping the water out whilst also allowing my sweat to evaporate, as it was a warm morning. After slogging into the wind as far as Treales I whizzed up to Inskip, then headed south to the cafe, looking forward to communing with my fellow full-time cyclists for the first time. They needn't know that I'd done so few miles, of course, and maybe I'd find a suitable riding companion on my very first day.

After leaning my bike against the wall I knocked the drops off my helmet and squelched towards the door, which I found firmly locked.

"Dammit, Simon!" I growled. "Double dammit," I added on seeing that the place only opened from Thursdays to Sundays. I suddenly felt very wet indeed, so I lost no time in hitting the road and by imagining myself to be leading the Paris-Roubaix race I reached the velodrome, or rather my estate, in record time. After a shower and a spot of lunch I changed only one of the worn tap washers and shook the crumbs from the toaster, as it made no sense to do all my jobs right away, before settling down at the computer to find a solution to my new cycling dilemma; what to do on rainy days when the cafe wasn't open.

It wasn't long before I discovered the world of turbo trainers, to which you attach your bike and replicate the cycling experience in the comfort of your own home. Back in the day I'd occasionally used simple rollers on which you had to get going by leaning on something or someone and pedal pretty fast to avoid falling off, so these modern turbos seemed like a vast improvement and just the job for doing a few miles in inclement weather. I soon saw that their prices ranged from about eighty pounds to over a thousand for ones with built in power meters – whatever they were – and plenty more bells and whistles besides. A little confused by this immense price disparity, because some of the cheaper ones had received excellent reviews, I sent Simon a text asking him what type I should buy. He replied about half an hour later:

Buy NONE of them until at least November.

Why not? I wrote back.

Turbos are for WINTER. Now you can ride every fine day and do SOMETHING ELSE when it rains. Do not get OBSESSED by cycling.

All right, Simon, keep your HAIR on.

Realising that he was right, once again, I pushed turbo trainers to the back of my mind and went to clean my filthy bike, before realising that I didn't yet know how to do it in the modern way, so after giving it a quick wipe I returned to the laptop and did some more research. Oh, what a lot of bike cleaning and maintenance products I found to feast my eyes upon! In the old days I'd made do with a bucket of soapy water and any old brush, before lubricating the chain and a few other moving parts with 3-in-1 or some other general purpose oil. After viewing a few in-depth videos I realised I needed a variety of brushes for different parts of the bike, bike-friendly detergent, specialist wet-lube and dry-lube, an ingenious contraption for cleaning the chain, a professional bike stand, a state of the art foot pump, and a whole gamut of tools. Many bike parts are secured by means of simple Allen keys, but it turned out that I now had to possess either pre-set torque wrenches or one incorporating a *newton meter*, for pity's sake, before daring to adjust a single thing.

Flabbergasted, I texted Simon again and he soon replied.

When adjusting things I use my hand and my brain to determine the tightness. Get off that damned computer before you spend a fortune on things you don't need.

What the hell is dry-lube? I replied.

The latest way to make money from obsessive cyclists. Just oil your chain. Now, please let me mend some teeth.

OK, thanks.

Another ping. *Don't forget to defrost the lamb chops*, I read, but this one came from Sarah. I'd momentarily forgotten that she rarely left Simon's side at work, so I shoved the chops in the microwave and prepared myself for a spot of scolding at dinner time, which I got.

"If you keep this up Simon's going to bill you for the next batch of rubber gloves," she said over the slightly burnt chops and soggy vegetables, as despite having spent my working life in and out of hotel kitchens I still couldn't cook to save my life.

My eyes questioned her, as my mouth was busy with the tough meat.

"Dentists can't just pick up their phones then shove their hand back in a patient's gob, you know. Simon's told me to warn you not to spend too much time online, or you'll end up with a garage full of bikes like him."

I suppressed a smile and nodded meekly.

"Which we're not going to have, are we?"

I lowered my eyes and shook my head.

"Because we aren't nearly as well off as him, are we?"

"No, love."

"Oh, and he told me to tell you that Roots Cafe only opens from Thursday to Sunday."

"I found that out for myself today."

"And he's set you a little task. When you go cycling you're to make a mental note of what type of people have what type of bike, then report back to him on Sunday."

"How strange, but I'll do it."

She grinned slyly. "We have our reasons."

Roots was by no means the only cafe within riding distance, so after being an exemplary house-husband the next day – mainly due to the rain – I cycled to Scorton by way of Pilling and Cockerham on Wednesday. In olden times the Priory Cafe was usually chock-a-block with cyclists every weekend. We'd drink gallons of tea and maybe buy a butty or a cake if we were feeling flush, before retrieving our bikes from the piles of them leant against the walls. That day, however, on stepping over the threshold I could see it had changed beyond recognition. The midweek clientele seemed aged and rather prosperous, judging by the succulent meals they were tucking into, and there wasn't a pot of tea or a plate of beans on toast in sight. Already feeling hesitant about adding my sweaty presence to this gathering of mostly corpulent oldies, when the young waitress told me I couldn't lean my bike on the railings outside – the only place I could keep an eye on it – I decided to take my business across the way to a thriving establishment situated in a converted barn. As well as a large gift shop, a small garden centre and a spacious restaurant, I found a lovely covered patio to the rear and lost no time in leaning my bike alongside a few others and taking a seat a near a trio of fit-looking young riders.

They returned my greeting in a friendly manner before resuming their conversation about a recent race they'd done. They clearly belonged to some kind of racing team because they sported matching kit and carbon bikes almost as expensive as Simon's, as by then my online research had made me au fait with most of the bike brands from Alchemy through to Zinn, although I had no intention of incurring Sarah's wrath by buying another one; not yet, anyway. While sipping my tea and munching the bacon butty which the waiter had been happy to serve me – this being a cyclist and walker-friendly place, unlike the snobby dump across the road – I occasionally glanced over at the lads, but none of them saw fit to include me in their by now more general cycling chat.

At first I suspected them of passive ageism or simple ignorance, but on leaning down to loosen my shoes I came face to face with something which set me apart from them far more than our forty-year age difference. My bike was a fine one, my clothing stylish and close-fitting, the excess fat I still carried barely noticeable, and my leg muscles increasingly well-defined, but... oh, they were still hairy! As most of my remaining readers will surely know, all racing cyclists shave their legs. Many club riders do too, as it's part of the aesthetics of the sport, though I'd noticed that Simon and his pals didn't bother. My legs aren't overly hirsute, so it wasn't something I'd given much thought to, but might these athletic young fellows be cutting me due to this unmistakable badge – or badges – of the non-serious cyclist?

Had my legs been silky-smooth they might have mistaken me for a grizzled racing veteran, perhaps even a former pro, and graced me with a comment or two. I could have mentioned the time trials I used to compete in less than a mile from where we were sitting – up and down the A6 – and we might have compared and contrasted our different eras or the advances in cycling technology for a while, before they whizzed off to complete their training ride and I pottered home, content to have made contact with the latest generation of competitors. When they stood up to leave, their tanned legs lithe and hairless, I swear that one of them cast a glance at my unshorn ones and winced, so after they'd gone every time I looked at them they seemed hairier. Riding home I kept glancing down and by the time I reached Fulwood I felt like some kind of human mammoth, pushing the pedals with my positively woolly limbs.

Later in the shower I was sorely tempted to set to with my razor, but I was afraid how Sarah might react to this radical and frankly unnecessary action, not to mention the scorn and/or ridicule Simon would subject me to on Sunday, before his hairy legs powered him into the distance up the first convenient climb. Safely out of the shower with my manliness intact, I then remembered some electric clippers with which Sarah had occasionally cut my hair. I found them in a drawer and selected an attachment that I believed would trim the hairs down to a length which would lead other serious cyclists to believe that I'd merely delayed my latest shave, surely no great sin for a long-retired racer. It seemed like such a brilliant idea that I donned a pair of shorts and scampered out onto the patio, where I clipped my legs from ankle to mid-thigh, which looked a bit daft, so I did a few more inches before rushing inside to take a peek in the full-length mirror. From a distance they looked fine, but on closer inspection I saw that the dratted clippers had left patches of longer hairs all over the place. I was about to oil the metal parts and start again, but on looking up I saw my worried expression in the mirror. My face hardened.

"I *am* a proper cyclist and I *will* shave my legs," I said aloud after staring myself out. Without more ado I hopped back into the shower and spent the best part of an hour there until not a single hair remained, not even behind the knees, the trickiest place of all.

I dressed and got downstairs just as Sarah was opening the door.

"Had a good day, love?"

"Middling." She gazed at me. "What have you been up to?"

"Oh, I rode to Scorton and stopped at a nice cafe there. We could drive over sometime if you like. They sell plants and jam and... why are you looking at me like that?"

"Had you been fifty years younger I'd have suspected you of pinching change from my purse."

"Eh?"

"You look like a little boy who's just done something naughty."

I rubbed my flushed right cheek, then the left one. "Ah, yes, well, I've been busy tinkering with my bike, so I haven't started making dinner yet."

She shook the bag containing the takeaway pizza she'd agreed to pick up on the way home.

"Ah, that explains it. I mean, I thought I had to peel spuds and whatnot, but subconsciously I must have known that I... didn't... have... to." My voice had tailed off because she wasn't buying it. I took the bag and hurried into the kitchen.

She followed. "Let me guess. You've bought some expensive cycling-related item and you're ashamed or afraid to tell me."

I sighed and nodded slowly. "I saw a bike a bit like Simon's at Scorton, then when I got back I was looking at it online and before I knew it I'd pressed the buy button."

Her ironic smile was replaced by a look of thorough indignation, then she steadied herself against the table. "How much?" she croaked.

"Er, not quite as much as Simon's."

"Oh, my God. He told me something like this would happen, but I expected you to at least have the decency to try to talk me round before spending... how many thousand?"

I looked at my hand, then held it up with the fingers neatly splayed.

"Five?" she whimpered.

I slowly raised the other hand and was about to count off a few fingers, but instead I patted her cheeks, stepped back, and pulled down my fleece bottoms.

"Ta-dahhh!" I cried. "No, not my snazzy boxers. Lower down."

"Ah, I see."

I flexed my quads. "Every cyclist worth his salt shaves his legs, you see."

She nodded. "Yes, Simon told me you'd probably do it soon. Right, rustle up a salad and pop the pizza in the microwave for a couple of minutes." She made for the stairs.

I scurried after her. "So don't you mind?"

"Why should I?

"And, er... if I had bought an expensive bike, what then?"

She turned and looked down at me. "Then your life wouldn't have been worth living for a very long time. Salad."

"Yes, love."

Later we sat out on the patio for a while and my legs tingled in a very agreeable way.

"Will you be riding tomorrow, Tom?"

"Yes, I expect so, but I must remember to taper for Sunday."

"To what?"

"To taper my rides. You know, to do less each day, so I'll be raring to go on Sunday, when I mean to show Simon and his mates a... er..."

She smiled. "A clean pair of legs?"

"I wish. No, just that I'm a little bit fitter and they soon won't have to wait for me on the climbs."

"Well, I'm glad you're enjoying it."

I took her hand. "And I'm glad you and Simon convinced me to give it a go. If truth be told I believe I would have been at a loose end this week without the bike." I shaded my eyes, because the waning sun was illuminating our decrepit shed.

She chuckled. "Don't worry about that old thing. I'm sure it'll stay upright for another year."

"Oh, I'll fix the roof soon. It's only my first week, after all."

"Yes. I wonder though… what is all your training really leading to?"

In such a question coming from Sarah I perceived Simon's influence, as they had plenty of time to chat at work every day, and no doubt my cycling was the Theme of the Week.

"Well, it's just leading to greater fitness, so I can ride further… and faster, without getting too tired to mend sheds and things."

"Don't you have a specific goal then?"

"Nope. Should I?"

"Oh, I don't know. I'm glad you don't appear to be riding down the slippery slope to the kind of obsession you had in your twenties, but we… I guess you'll probably need something to set your sights on."

"Like what?"

Oh, I don't know. An especially long ride to somewhere interesting, perhaps. Something you'll strive towards, then feel satisfied when you've achieved it."

"What has Simon been saying?"

"Oh, nothing in particular. We natter a lot about this and that. Ah, and don't forget to make a mental note of what type of people have what type of bike."

"I haven't forgotten. Today there were three very fit lads on three very fast bikes, and an elderly couple on an elderly tandem, so all was as it should be."

She shrugged. "Keep observing."

6

It wasn't until my short ride to Roots Cafe on Saturday morning that I cottoned on to what Simon must be driving at. By eleven there were at least a score of cyclists seated in the spacious patio, but as their bikes were leaning on every available wall I couldn't tell who their owners were. As I slowly sipped my coffee, sharing a picnic table with a few lads from the Pendle Forest cycling club, I observed the ebb and flow and noticed that generally speaking the keen club riders possessed modern carbon mounts costing between two and five thousand pounds, while a jolly group of older fellows sported vintage steel bikes, stylish relics of the seventies and eighties such as Italian Colnagos and Bianchis with expensive Campagnolo components which had stood the test of time. One happy, chattering group of relative newbies were equipped with bikes from Ribble Cycles and Halfords – the Boardman models – which probably cost about a grand and were perfectly adequate for their needs, or mine for that matter.

So all was as it should be, I thought, until I identified the owner of a top of the range BMC race bike, as used by Greg Van Avermaet in his successful classics campaign of the previous season. Unlike the powerful Belgian, the short chap in his fifties who proudly grasped the gold and grey 'Teammachine' wouldn't be winning the Paris-Roubaix any time soon, because his belly almost touched the top tube when he mounted and he wobbled along for about thirty yards before finally managing to clip his feet into the pedals. His legs were hairy too, and he was riding alone, so I had to feel sorry for the poor deluded chap who'd probably believed that by shelling out about ten grand he would ingratiate himself with the cycling community, when in actual fact he cut an incongruous and rather silly figure, although to be honest only I appeared to have paid him much attention.

I then set my sights on a beautiful Pinarello Dogma F10, a mouth-watering machine whose owner turned out to be a bearded bloke of about my age, dressed in the trendy dull-coloured clothes that I already abhorred. I strolled over to the open gate again to observe his departure and although the man looked quite fit I could tell from his posture that he hadn't been riding a bike for long, as his shoulders were stiff, his handlebars too high, his saddle a tad too low, and his legs too thin and hairy.

No-one else seemed to have noticed him, though I believe my table companions had begun to wonder why I kept jumping up and striding to the gate, before returning with a smirk on my face, so when the small Trek Emonda SLR was collected I sat tight as a beefy lady of about forty-five mounted it. After a large Wilier Superleggera had been wheeled away by a snooty-looking chap whose pretty wife possessed a Specialized S-Works rather like Simon's, I decided to conclude my research for the day.

I glanced at my own bike and smiled, because I felt it was just right for me. The bare metal frame seemed discreet beside all the colourful carbon models and although a few years old it was every bit as effective as any other bike there. What it lacked in lightness it made up for in comfort, titanium being a supremely forgiving material, and I felt a surge of renewed gratitude that my friend had seen fit to give it to me. Yes, that was the bike for me all right, and as I could affix and remove the mudguards quite easily I saw no reason to buy another one in the foreseeable future. Yes, in three or four years' time I'd have become a familiar sight on the roads and at the cafes, an inveterate mile-eater who eschewed the caprices of cycling fashion but could certainly shift when he had a mind to.

'*That's Tom Eastham,*' I imagined one admirer saying.

'*Fit-looking bloke. Does he race?*'

'*Not now. He used to be quite handy back in the day, but now he just rides for fun. One day he came past me up the Trough like a bloody gazelle. You wouldn't think he was sixty-odd.*'

'*Old bike though.*'

'*Ha, God knows how fast he'd go with carbon wheels and whatnot. He's a real phenomenon…*'

I shook my head to dispel this ludicrous fantasy and I was about to leave when a curious sight made me resume my seat and sip the dregs of my coffee. I suppose there's nothing all that unusual about seeing a man on a touring bike, with panniers fore and aft and a big saddlebag too, but as none of the other bikes were carrying anything larger than a slightly bulky saddle pack he certainly stood out from the crowd. The slim, balding chap looked a bit younger than me and sported a deep suntan, a thick grizzled beard and plenty more hair on his muscular legs, which was just fine, because he wasn't one of us, but a tourist, and a pretty serious one by the look of things. As well as two water bottles within the frame he carried a third one *under* the down tube, which tickled me pink for some reason. His bike was a white Kona model with a sturdy leather saddle, disc brakes, a triple chainset, and an extra-wide range of rear sprockets to enable him to get up steep climbs with all that stuff weighing him down. I deduced from the rolled up foam mat on the front pannier rack that he was carrying camping gear and I felt an almost overpowering urge to speak to this hardy adventurer.

As the Pendle Forest lads had just left I could offer him a pew, but another club group were dismounting, so I boldly beckoned the fellow, who happened to be looking at his phone. I saw that the other new arrivals had ridden all the way from Keighley, about fifty miles away, so they certainly deserved to rest their weary legs and might also have a tale to tell, but I'd set my heart on the intrepid tourist and when he finally looked up I waved cheerily and urged him to make haste towards the only free table, which he did.

His blue eyes perused me over his plain sunglasses. "Er, do I know you?" he asked in a soft Scottish accent.

"Ha, no, but I guess you'll be keen to rest after your long ride, and the other tables are full." I moved my empty mug to the edge of ours. "I was just about to order something, but you go in first while I hold the fort, ha ha."

He eyed me shrewdly, seeming unsure if he'd just met the village idiot or a potential bike thief. "You order first, if you like, while I sort some stuff out."

"All right." I placed my helmet and gloves on the table and stood up. "Shall I get yours too while I'm at it?"

"All right. I'll have a white coffee, please."

"Is that all, after so many miles?"

He smiled. "I've just come from a campsite up the road. Easy day today."

"I see. Won't be a mo." By hobbling speedily around to the cafe on my cleated shoes I was able to beat the Keighley lads to the counter and soon returned to find the globetrotter with both pairs of pannier bags on the seat and the table full of stuff. I waved away his offer to pay for the coffee and asked him what he was doing.

He chuckled. "Trying to redistribute the weight. The front end felt too light, so I added more heavy stuff, but I think I overdid it. It's my first real tour, you see, so I'm still a bit clueless."

Rather than feeling disappointed that he was a rookie rather than a seasoned veteran, I warmed to the stranger even more, because what he was doing wasn't a million miles from what I could also possibly do in the not too distant future, given a certain amount of determination, expense, and the green light from Sarah. Him being Scottish had reminded me that in early August my wife and I were driving to Banavie, near Fort William, with some friends whose cousin owned a house there. We'd be staying for a week and I'd already planned to take the bike along to do a few rides, but a new and far more exciting idea had occurred to me. I waited patiently while he buckled the bags, then introduced myself.

He shook my outstretched hand. "Hi, Tom. I'm Rob."

"Tell me about your trip, Rob," I said, rather than peppering him with questions.

It turned out that he'd left his home in Dumfries four days earlier and ridden through the Lake District and the Forest of Bowland, before reaching the flatlands and realising that he was exhausted. His preparation prior to the trip consisted of a few hundred miles on a lightweight bike, rather like me, but his relatively high daily mileage on the fully loaded tourer had worn him out.

"So I'll have an easy day today, then carry on south to Wales. I'm going to ride through Snowdonia and mid-Wales to the Brecon Beacons, then make my way east to my son's house in Gloucester."

I nodded eagerly. "And then ride home?"

He laughed. "Not on your life! I'll have had enough by then. My wife'll be there and I'll drive home with her."

The similarity of his trip to the one that was taking shape in my mind was uncanny and surely destiny had brought us together, I firmly believed. I then told him about my projected ride to Banavie as if I'd been planning it for some time.

"That'll be a nice trip, especially if you avoid Glasgow and Edinburgh. I've found that the busy bits are the downside of touring. From here to Wales it's going to be a bit of a bore. I'll avoid the main roads as much as I can, but I'll still have to ride through a lot of towns. Still, at least it'll be fairly flat for a while. Will you be camping too?"

"Er, I'm not sure yet." I glanced at the bike which he'd leant against our private table.

He sighed. "If I could turn back the clock I think I'd do things a bit differently."

"How?"

"Well, I'm fully equipped to camp, and I've camped twice, but towards the end of a long day when you see a bed and breakfast sign it's just too tempting to check in, shower, have a meal at a pub or nip to the chippy, then sleep in a comfy bed."

Although this made sense, especially for a first tour, I felt a little disappointed, as it would mean less gear and I loved the look of his bike. "I see. Without the camping gear, how many bags would you need?"

"Oh, for this trip I reckon I'd make do with the rear panniers."

I pictured the bike like that and it wasn't nearly so impressive. "Just a pair of panniers, yes," I mumbled.

"On the other hand, if you don't want to tie yourself to an itinerary, which I don't, there's always a chance that you'll find no room at the inn, especially in midsummer when you go, so I think a happy medium would be to carry a small sleeping bag, a bivvy bag, a tiny stove and a few provisions, in case you have to sleep out."

I perked up, because all the bags were back in place, though not quite as stuffed full as his were. "Yes, yes, that sounds like the best idea. How... how much did your bike cost?"

"Just over a thousand."

I almost yelped for joy. Only a thousand! The lighter wheels I'd been tempted to buy for my bike cost more than that, as the price of top-end components is truly prohibitive. So, the bike, the bags, the camping gear, and above all that third water bottle cage, which I'd simply have to have, wouldn't set me back all that much, not compared to pointless upgrades for the boringly naked bike I now possessed. I strove to contain my excitement and steer my mind away from this essentially secondary element of the bicycle touring experience.

"What's it like?" I asked him.

"What's what like?"

"Being on a bike tour. I mean, I did a few forty-odd years ago, but I've forgotten how the daily routine feels," I said truthfully, as I mostly remembered the bad times, like puncturing half way up Hardknott Pass in the pouring rain, almost being flattened by a drunken driver in Chester, and a few more grim moments. That's not to say that I didn't have good memories too, but they were very fuzzy after so many years.

He sipped his coffee and eyed the cloudy sky. "For me I think it's something I'm going to appreciate more when I've finished."

"Oh, right."

"I say that now because I've tired myself out, my arse is sore, and I'm not especially looking forward to the next forty or so miles, until I get south of the Mersey, but I've realised that you have to take the rough with the smooth on a place to place tour, especially in this crowded country." He shrugged. "I suppose everything worth doing has its downsides, or there'd be no sense of achievement. Well, I'd better get back on the road."

"Where are you staying tonight?"

He smiled wearily. "I suppose I'll push on and try to get to Cheshire, then find a hotel or a B&B somewhere quiet. I really can't be bothered with the tent tonight."

I offered to accompany him through Preston, avoiding the busier roads.

"Thanks, that's kind of you."

I managed to make our urban journey last almost an hour and we probably incurred more risks on the streets and avenues – what with folk stepping out and drivers opening their doors – than if we'd ridden straight through on the main road. On finally reaching Penwortham we pulled over and I suggested he ride on to Lostock Hall.

"At least I think that's best, but it'll be quite busy whichever way you go," I said, feeling slightly stressed after our rather draining odyssey.

"I'll be fine, and tomorrow I'll be in the Welsh hills, so what the hell."

"Yes. I suppose my trip will be quieter."

"Hmm, yes, but there aren't all that many roads in the Highlands, so you'll often be sharing them with cars and caravans. Still, the rough with the smooth, eh?"

"Yes." We shook hands and I watched him ride away. On his imposing bike the cars seemed to give him plenty of room, but I was having minor doubts about this place to place touring business. On setting off back, however, the memory of his third water bottle – essential when crossing deserts, steppes and suchlike – cheered me up somewhat, and after riding straight through Preston on the main road I began to feel more sanguine, because the cars had kept their distance, and didn't thousands of people commute in cities every day?

"The rough with the smooth," I muttered as I rolled onto the driveway, before vowing not to begin to babble about my brave new plan right away.

My talented wife was practising a piece on her violin, so after greeting her silently I showered quickly, scoffed a pork pie, then opened the laptop, eager to delve into the world of touring bikes. I soon found myself on the website of a large bicycle retailer which happened to have a shop in Preston. Perhaps it was just as well that they didn't have any suitable models in stock or I might have jumped in the car and found myself saddled with a bike which wasn't quite right. Acquiring new things is a pleasure to be savoured, after all, so I settled down to do some serious research, until my sneaky spouse caught me in the act.

"What are you looking at now?" she murmured over my shoulder, having crept into our little study like an especially silent panther.

I turned around and closed the laptop in one smooth movement. "Had a good practice?"

"Yes. Well?"

"What?"

"What were those bags you were perusing with such rapt attention?"

"Well, this morning I... I had a brainwave. I'm thinking of cycling up to Banavie. I may also ride back, but we'll see how the outward leg goes first." I smiled proudly. "What do you think of that then?"

"Simon and I were wondered if it would occur to you."

"Ah, I see."

"Yes, he said it was the right sort of distance and would be something for you to get your teeth into, rather than just getting them into bacon butties in different cafes every day, which you'll soon get bored of. His words, not mine."

"Ah, thus the hints about specific goals and whatnot."

She smiled. "That's right, and it'll make for a better holiday too, as you'll want to take it easy before riding back, although Simon believes you'll have had enough and will come back in the car."

I stiffened. "Does he now?"

"Yes, he thinks that after three hundred miles on a loaded bike you'll not want to repeat the experience for some time."

"Ha! He underestimates me."

"He believes you'll be happy to return the bike for the time being and get back on your lightweight one."

"What do you mean, return the bike? To the shop? I don't think they'd take kindly to that somehow."

She ruffled my hair. "He'll lend you his touring bike, of course."

I frowned. "That old thing?"

"It's got new tyres, a new chain, and new... cogs or something."

"Gosh, you must have spent every spare moment chattering about me all week."

She shrugged. "It's made a change."

"No, I'm afraid that old bike won't do, love."

"Why not?"

If I'd mentioned the lack of a third water bottle cage under the down tube she wouldn't have understood, so I racked my brain for a convincing reason to buy a new bike. "Because I'm... it's a bit small for me, and... well, I think touring's something I'm going to really enjoy, and besides, it's better to have a cheaper bike for the winter, as the salt from the roads can corrode them and I want to look after my titanium bike," I babbled.

"He said you'd say something like that."

"I might have guessed."

"Talk it over with him tomorrow."

"Yes, love."

"But in the meantime don't go making any rash purchases."

"No, love."

As she left the room I opened the laptop.

"We'll drive round to my mother's shortly," she said from the doorway.

Thwarted, I closed it again.

7

The following day we enjoyed a mostly sunny fifty-odd mile ride and it bothered me not a jot when they distanced me on the longer climbs, because I soon caught them up over the top, and who cared about speed anyway? After riding north-west through Chipping and Dunsop Bridge to Wigglesworth, we returned by way of Chatburn and Longridge, before Simon and I repaired to Roots Cafe for a bite to eat. On recalling where Rob the Scotsman had leant his wonderful bike I admitted that meeting him had sparked my sudden desire to go touring.

He nodded. "That's often the way, and I must admit that whenever I see a fully loaded tourer I experience a strong urge to sell up and take to the road."

"Can't you do a tour in your holidays?"

"No, Sue wouldn't stand for it, and I don't blame her. I'm out on the bike every Sunday and some Saturdays as it is, plus an evening or two in the summer months. I suppose I could squeeze in a week a year, but what's the point of that? I want to set off and ride… well, a long, long way."

"What, like around the world?"

He sipped his coffee and shook his head. "No, I'd prefer to do one continent at a time."

I gawped at him, then found my voice. "One continent at a time, yes, that sounds more reasonable."

"Yes."

"Are you serious?"

"Yes."

"But you've never mentioned this to me before."

He shrugged. "I think it's best not to harp on about things until you're sure you're going to do them, but two years from now I'd like to be in… Slovenia, for instance, making my way towards the Black Sea."

"Right. Does Sue know about this?"

"She knows I want to do long tours, but I think she imagines I'll ride to John o' Groats or somewhere like that. Still, it won't matter too much when I'm retired, as we'll be together the rest of the time, but keep this to yourself for the time being. She worries about the traffic when I'm out, so I don't particularly want her to picture me up the Khyber Pass until I'm there."

"No, not until you're there." I imagined him pedalling past groups of rifle-toting brigands with his massive panniers and three or even four water bottles. "My trip to Scotland seems like a ride in the park now."

He chuckled. "Yes, but you're probably going to do it, while I'm just… well, not exactly fantasising, as I'm serious about doing some lengthy tours, but until I go it'll just be so much hot air."

"The same for me till I actually set off to Scotland about a month from now."

"I envy you, though we're going to Iceland for ten days, so that'll be fun too." He rubbed his hands together. "Right, let's talk bikes."

My fingers tingled, as the previous evening I'd been tickling the laptop keyboard while Sarah watched TV, something I'd had less time for since resuming my cycling career, although the number of cycling-related videos I'd watched more than made up for it. I told Simon about all the touring bike reviews I'd read and how I'd reached the conclusion that a medium-priced, steel-framed model would be best.

"I agree. A bike's a bike, after all, and when you're carrying luggage there's little point in shaving off ounces here and there."

"I might buy a Genesis Tour de Fer, because… well I like the name and the simple colour scheme."

"How about a Claud Butler like mine?"

I wrinkled my nose. "Well, they're a bit old hat and… that."

"What?"

I sighed. "Yours doesn't have mounts for a third water bottle."

"So? Just stick another bottle in one of the bags."

I confessed to my infatuation with the unusually positioned bottle.

He laughed. "You wouldn't think you were sixty years old."

My grizzled head fell. "I know."

"But I'm the same, or worse." He pointed at his bike. "That's a world-class racing machine that Sagan or Alaphilippe would be happy to ride just as it is, but I'm already looking at forthcoming models to replace it." He scratched his head and seemed nonplussed for once. "Then again, I forget that in two years' time my cycling life will change forever. I suppose our enthusiasm is a bit childish in a way, but who wants to act their age anyway?"

I grinned. "Exactly. If you give me the nod I'll order that Genesis bike right away."

"Is it in stock then?"

"Yes, in more than one place. Ah, in a few days my touring career can begin, with a few trial runs."

He perused a crust of his sausage butty, then pushed the plate away. "Come round to mine later."

"Why?"

"You'll see."

The following morning I wobbled along our cul-de-sac much as I'd done about two action-packed months ago, but this time it wasn't lack of practice that made me unstable, but the sixty pounds of bike and bags which I sat astride. Simon had insisted that before ordering my bike, racks, bags and other touring accoutrements I ought to get the hang of his old Claud Butler. He had an inkling that I was more enamoured of the *idea* of bicycle touring and its trappings than the reality of riding a stonking great bike up hill and down dale for days on end. So, he'd pressed his faithful old tourer upon me and told me to fill the bags and do at least one longish ride before committing myself to that unglamorous and potentially onerous branch of the sport.

I'd loaded the front and rear panniers with all sorts of things from the house and garage, such as towels and tools and a few bits of wood. I'd also strapped an old tent to the rear pannier rack, hoping that its presence might inspire me to wish to sleep in one, as I couldn't justify the purchase of a modern lightweight shelter if I wasn't going to use it. Rob's idea of taking only emergency camping gear had sounded all right at the time, but would I really fancy sleeping under a hedge in a bivvy bag? I doubted it somehow, and one-man tents are so light these days that I thought I ought to get one. Sarah had set me a spending limit of £2000 and as the bike would cost no more than £1200, plus about two hundred for the panniers and racks, I could also afford to buy a tent, a sleeping bag, lightweight cooking tackle and whatever other indispensable items I was likely to read about.

Simon had told me that when he came to conquer his first continent he intended to camp most of the time, you see, and I wanted my Scottish tour to replicate his proposed adventures to some extent, because I was already hoping that he'd invite me along. Yes, I'd been severely bitten by the touring bug without leaving the comfort of my home, but before I'd left the estate I'd begun to get cold feet despite the warm morning. The bike was so heavy and unwieldy that I was tempted to nip back and ditch the electric drill and other tools I'd shoved in the rear panniers, but as they were my camping gear substitutes I had no option but to soldier on. Once on the lanes I began to breathe more freely, but not for long, because the effort required to propel that burdensome bike soon had me panting like an overheated spaniel. Being passed by a couple of mature riders from the Ribble Valley club didn't help matters, because I instinctively tried to keep up with them, until a scarcely perceptible rise made me ease off and begin to see the light. Simon's bike sported heavy, puncture-resistant tyres which alone must have slowed me down by at least two miles an hour, and the loaded bike weighed about three times as much as mine. I rolled to a halt and leant it against a convenient bench, before walking across the lane and gazing over a gate.

The freshly mown field made me see things through fresh eyes. Simon had forbidden me from watching more bicycle touring videos online, because he insisted they would give me preconceived ideas and fill my mind with idyllic images which might undermine or dilute my own experience, but I'd already seen a few before the ban was imposed and I recalled a short one about a couple cycling through the Cotswolds. In it they rolled gaily along without a care in the world, chatting, enjoying the views, and pedalling whenever they felt like it. On a steep hill they used their super-low gears for a while, before climbing off and pushing their bikes. At the time I'd thought, gosh, their average speed must be down into single figures and they can't get far that way, but a short bout of simple arithmetic told me that in a full day's easy riding one could still cover a heck of a lot of miles.

So it was that I strolled across the lane and before remounting I moved the chain from the large chainring to the middle one. After wiping the remaining sweat from my forehead I inhaled the balmy air, got my leg over the bulky bags, and set off again, but this time I set myself the task of moving along with the least possible effort. I was amazed by what a doddle cycling could be if I put my mind to it! On cresting the rise the lane looked pan-flat, but by ceasing to pedal I found that I was in fact descending, so I coasted down the slope at jogging pace until I was forced to resume my minimal exertions. I'd planned to do only a short ride that day, as I was tired after our Sunday ride, but on discovering how efficient the bicycle could be I decided to head over towards Beacon Fell after all. So this is why cycling became such an instant hit in the late-nineteenth century, I thought, because it's so damned easy! Just then I felt I could ride all day long and into the night if need be, but it took me so long to reach St Michael's on Wyre that I realised that a compromise between speed and sloth had to be found if I were to reach Banavie in less than a fortnight.

So I sped up a bit, but that super-slow stretch had effectively reprogrammed my mind and I was now able to potter along quite happily at an estimated speed of ten or eleven miles an hour. After passing over the motorway near Bilsborrow the road began to rise into the hills and I gleefully engaged the smallest of the three chainrings. As the steepness increased I changed up the rear sprockets and found it most amusing to be pedalling freely while travelling at less than walking pace. Over the years I had occasionally hoisted my flabby arse onto a mountain bike to go for a short spin, so these extreme gears weren't entirely new to me, but it was good fun to propel a total weight of about 240 pounds up a hill with so little effort. It did make the hill last rather a long time, of course, but this enabled me to take in the sights, sounds and smells of the countryside far more fully than when I was swinging my titanium bike from side to side in a desperate attempt to keep the much harder bottom gear moving. In the end I left Beacon Fell to my right and soon began to descend to the pretty village of Chipping, taking care on several curves not to end up in the hedge, as on the downhills my heavy steed gathered speed at an alarming rate, so I hoped that the modern disc brakes fitted to my forthcoming bike would have more stopping power than traditional calipers.

I found only one bike outside the often cyclist-filled Cobbled Corner Cafe – at the time of writing closed for refurbishment or forever – but it was of a type I hadn't expected to see so far from the main roads. Modern time trial bikes are extremely sleek, aerodynamic affairs with low-slung handlebars and deep-rimmed carbon wheels. Had I possessed one of those in my day... well, who knows what sort of world-beating times I'd have done, but back then we merely used the lightest possible wheels and sometimes a single chainring in order to dispense with the front derailleur, while figure-hugging lycra skin-suits were only affordable right at the end of my career, so I never tried one. The biggest single advance of all was the adoption of the handlebar extensions first used in triathlons which, by keeping the arms close together, enable the rider to cut through the air like a knife.

I admired the state-of-the-art machine for a while and imagined myself hurtling along the A6 upon it. My shaven legs then began to tingle as I had my latest impetuous brainwave. Could I, at sixty years of age, with a high-tech bike like that, plus an aerodynamic helmet and all the rest of the speed-enhancing accessories, possibly aspire to get near the times I'd achieved in my twenties? One day Simon had idly mentioned that oldsters were doing surprisingly swift times on the faster courses, but he'd put it down to super-smooth tarmac, heavy traffic, and the technology I'd just been ogling.

I looked from one bike to the other and dismissed this vainglorious fantasy from my mind. What if, after many months of excruciating training, I could match the times I'd done on a conventional bike wearing a cotton jersey and with the wind whistling through my then abundant hair? What would it prove? I gazed at the loaded tourer and smiled. No, this was the way to go, pedalling serenely along through leafy glens and past endless lochs, having profound thoughts and acting my age for once, not whizzing along a busy road looking like an ageing turkey packed in coloured cling film. I shook my head, then pushed open the door to find at the nearest table a tubby, ageing fellow packed into a matt-black skin-suit.

"Morning," I said to the ludicrous gent.

"Hi. Oh, is it… Tom?"

"Er, yes."

"Tom Eastham?"

"That's me."

"Ha, you haven't changed a bit, or not much. Take a seat."

Once seated I looked into his eyes but couldn't for the life of me remember who he was. He chortled on realising this and provided me with a view of his profile.

"Think back to… 1978, I think it was. The last twenty-five of the season on Brock and I'd set off a minute in front of you. I thought I was going to hold you off, then those bloody lights changed at Garstang and I had to stop. You got straight through and flippin' *flew* past me, but you helped to set my pace and I got under the hour for the first time. 59.55 I did that day and I believe you did 58.42, more or less."

I grasped my forehead. "Oh, let me think."

"I think you were fifth and won a fiver, but my memory's not what it was."

I slapped the table. "Bob! Bob Taylor." (Not his real name.)

"The same." We shook hands. "You did some cracking times for a couple more years, then I started to beat you. Never understood that."

I smiled bravely. "Oh, you know, my job, the girlfriend, the usual story. I eventually packed it in and only started riding again a couple of months ago."

He grinned. "Ah, yet another comeback man."

I shrugged. "I'm getting there."

After ordering coffee I glanced through the window at his super-bike and was glad that only the tip of my front wheel was visible. He was waiting for a toasted teacake, so I hoped to give a good account of myself, then slip away before he had chance to see the great lump of a bike I was on. I also wished to pick his brains about modern time trialling because, wavering wally that I am, I suddenly fancied having a go at it. That would come after my Anglo-Scottish tour, of course, or Sarah might think I was losing my marbles, but the sight of that bike must have joggled a certain cluster of brain cells, because I vividly saw myself upon one, hurtling along the A6 looking like Bradley Wiggins during his conquest of the hour record, or something like that.

"What's the time trial scene like nowadays, Bob?"

He shook his head and sighed. "Crippling."

"Crippling?"

"Yes, financially, I mean. Ah, it was much better back when you were riding. It was an even playing field then for anyone on a half-decent wage, but nowadays…" His teacake arrived and he bit into it savagely. "The wife's at the end of her tether… threatening to leave me," he went on as he munched. "That wind tunnel was the final straw, she said, and if I don't see sense she's off to Spain to live with her sister." He wiped the butter from his chin and took another bite. "But it had to be done… if I wanted to be competitive."

Once he'd dispatched the teacake he explained that his hideously expensive visit to a cycling-specific wind tunnel at Silverstone had resulted in some minor adjustments to his position which appeared to have improved his race times slightly.

"And I had this made to measure." He plucked at his skin-tight suit.

"That's a strange material."

"Yes, it's supposed to save me ten watts."

"What?"

"Watts." He smiled grimly. "We talk about saving watts these days rather than seconds." He then told me about the power meters he'd installed on three of his bikes and how he analysed the data after every ride. "So then I know exactly how many watts I can put out over a certain distance to get optimal results. That's the theory anyway."

My eyes must have rested on his paunch for a fraction too long, because he laughed and patted it. "I know what you're thinking, Tom. The winter before last I slimmed right down, but I lost strength too, so my times suffered. The funny thing is that the wind-tunnel bods said my belly wasn't such a bad thing, 'cause the wind flows past it quite nicely, so I shan't be going on another diet. I don't do hilly time trials anyway, and on the flat it doesn't affect my speed."

"So, er… what sort of times are you doing these days?"

He beamed. "About the same as thirty years ago."

"Really?"

"Yes, it's brilliant, isn't it? I did slow down a bit in my fifties, but when I started to embrace the new tech I got faster again. Last year I got under the hour on a fast course over in Yorkshire."

"That's great."

"Yeah, I was over the moon. It was a perfect day, mind you, as the winner did about forty-six minutes."

I gasped. "That fast!"

Oh, yes, and a couple of months ago some Polish guy got under forty-three minutes for the first time. That's almost thirty-five miles an hour. Some going."

This seemed to delight Bob rather than make him realise that his own times were positively pedestrian in comparison, but I still felt curious enough to ask him how much slower he thought he'd go on a conventional racing bike.

He puffed out his cheeks and expelled the air. "Oh, it doesn't bear thinking about. That's why I usually train on my TT bike."

"And on a normal bike with some of those clip-on tri-bars?" I said, still wondering if it would be worth having a go towards the end of the season.

"Well, they help a lot, but you'd still be at a massive disadvantage. No, what you need is…"

A few minutes later Bob had effectively ended my silly desire to test myself against the clock once more, as I'd have to spend at least two grand on a slightly outdated second-hand bike in order not to be a laughing stock. Were I to take it at all seriously I'd also need an expensive power meter for at least one bike, at which point my desire to save watts would entail unending expenditure as each new product superseded the old.

"Do you never feel like you're being taken for a ride, Bob?"

"In what way?"

"By the fact the manufacturers keep bringing out new things to force everyone to spend a ton of money every year."

He smiled. "Yes, deep down we all know it's a bit daft, but us testers (time trialists) have always been a funny lot. I mean, who in their right mind would get up at three in the morning and drive down to Wales to ride along a superfast dual-carriageway just to beat their time by a few seconds?" He shrugged. "Still, it's better than being some sad old bastard who spends every Sunday morning cleaning his car inside and out."

"That's true, but you ought to appease the wife a bit if you can."

"Bah, let her go to Spain if she wants, then I can train indoors as much as I like. The noise bothers her, you see."

"Training indoors? Oh, on one of those turbos, right."

He told me that most self-respecting testers did much of their training indoors, as the turbo replicates the race experience much better than most roads. "But I still come here now and then. I suppose old habits die hard. I'd better get going."

"Me too."

On stepping outside I held my breath.

Bob staggered on his cleats. "What the fuck is that, Tom?"

I grinned sheepishly and explained that I'd caught the touring bug. "So I'll be getting my own tourer before I ride to the Highlands in a few weeks."

He looked like he'd just eaten something rather nasty. "I... well, whatever floats your boat, mate, but how can you ride a... butcher's bike like that?"

I giggled. "Slowly. I'm trying to see cycling through fresh eyes, you see. So, much as I love the look of your aero machine, racing isn't a road I want to go down myself."

He nodded slowly, then smiled. "Hmm, I suppose a long tour won't do you any harm."

"Well, I hope not."

He patted the pannier containing the electric drill and bits of an old bird box. "Yes, as you're just starting back you'll need to get in plenty of miles before there's any point pushing yourself, and I don't suppose it matters if you do them on a... a thing like this." He pulled a cylindrical case from his single high-tech bottle cage and under an ultra-light inner tube found a rather mangled business card.

"Take this, Tom, and give me a call once you want to start training for time trials again."

"Thanks. Oh, yes, you're a plasterer. Still working, then?"

"Only in winter, now and then. It interferes too much with my training. Right, I'm heading down to Hesketh Lane."

"Me too, but don't worry, I'll follow in your aerodynamic wake."

After pumping my hand he jumped on and clattered off, as deep carbon-rimmed wheels seem to echo every bump in the road. I made haste to follow and after turning right at the pub I watched him hurtle off down the lane, already tucked into his aero position.

"Poor deluded fool," I muttered, and on seeing a litter bin I was tempted to stop and chuck his card into it, as the devil works in mysterious ways and I didn't want to fall into temptation at a later date. It wouldn't do to be so rude though, and our slightly humid spare room might benefit from damp-proofing and replastering at some point. I turned right at Hesketh Lane and resumed my super-slow riding up a long drag. Bob had just been a blip, a blast from the past, and I pushed him to the back of my cluttered mind. Besides, due to his obsession with speed he'd never tour entire continents like Simon... and maybe me.

8

So I ordered the bike, racks, panniers and plenty more bits and pieces from a large cycling retailer, before settling down to choose my lightweight camping gear. All told I spent a tad less than two thousand and Sarah sincerely hoped that I had everything I could possibly require for the rest of the year.

I planted a kiss on her smooth brow. "Of course, love. Thanks for being so understanding."

"Well, you have to get started on your retirement activities, but don't forget that our income isn't quite what it was."

"No, love."

"And we won't get our state pensions for a few years."

"No, love."

"In fact we ought to begin to plan our ongoing expenses from now on."

"Yes, love."

"Fortunately violins are quite low maintenance and my Cremona might well see me out, but I fear that cycling's always going to be a drain on our resources."

I erased an image of Bob's bike from my mind. "Oh, I don't think so. Tyres and other parts need replacing now and then, but none of them cost all that much."

She smiled. "Simon thinks we ought to agree on an annual cycling budget."

I frowned. "I see. So you're still spending every spare moment chattering about me."

"Well, what with the new bike and the Scotland trip, you're still a hot topic between patients."

I gasped. "Between the patients too?"

"I mean between patient and patient. So, Simon's suggested capping your cycling costs at two thousand per year."

My lips twitched, but I didn't smile. "Hmm, yes, that sounds reasonable. It's quite generous of you, in fact, as long as I can carry over any surplus from one year to the next."

"I don't see why not, but are you so sure there'll be a surplus?"

I pictured the two bikes I'd soon possess. "Oh, yes, I think so. Quite a big one, I hope."

"Don't forget all those bacon butties."

"Eh?"

"I didn't realise just how much all your cafe stops would add up to until Simon pointed it out to me."

"That was kind of him. And what approximate figure did he arrive at for this necessary consumption of essential calories?"

She explained that five bacon butties per week, at an approximate unit cost of a fiver, would come to about £1250 per year.

"I see."

"But I've decided to subtract the cost price of each butty – let's say a pound – so we're talking a thousand a year spent in cafes."

"You're forgetting my coffees and teas."

"No, I'm not. We reasoned that having a drink can be considered a non-cycling expense. Even I nip out for a coffee now and then, after all."

I then pictured my resplendent new bike which I meant to ride every day with the rear panniers attached. "I know! I'll take a flask and a butty with me and sit on a bench somewhere, soaking up the sun and conserving my cycling budget."

She chuckled. "I won't be too strict, but you see my point, don't you?"

"Yes, that a year's worth of butties adds up to the price of… something quite dear. Point taken, love."

When she picked up the remote I made for the door, but she called me back and suggested that we watch one of the many good programmes we had recorded.

"Er, well, I was just–"

"Sit down." She patted the sofa cushion. "Simon says that ogling cycling gear all the time is just as pointless and mind-numbing as watching TV. You've ordered everything you need for the time being, so try to break the habit."

"But I want to begin to plan my tour," I whined.

"Not yet. Simon says you ought to leave that till the week before. He says that you'll end up spending so much time on that street view thing that when you go you'll feel like you've already been."

"Oh, how daft…"

"And he knows, because he's already seen every single attraction in Iceland and regrets it."

I sat down. "Well, at least that proves he isn't infallible. Right, which gripping detective series are we going to watch then?"

"None." She clicked the play button and I happily settled down to watch *Ride of My Life: The Story of the Bicycle.*

When the huge box arrived the following Monday I lugged it into the garage and fell upon it like a greedy child on Christmas morn. On sliding out the shiny red bike I realised that it was the first entirely new one I'd possessed since being given a Carlton ten-speed machine on a real Christmas Day in 1974, as my parents hoped that my healthy new hobby would keep me out of mischief, which it did, because I didn't taste beer till I was seventeen and largely eschewed my friends' monumental piss-ups in favour of two lengthy rides every weekend. After the Carlton I bought a second-hand Reynold 531 frame from a club mate and built it up with new and used parts, and all my subsequent bikes were cobbled together in a similar manner, until now.

After flinging bits of foam and cardboard behind me I inserted the wheels, attached the handlebars and saddle, then stood back to admire the stylish steel bike upon which I planned to ride thousands of miles. I recalled that my Carlton had also been a reddish colour, so I felt that I'd come full circle after forty-four years. Then, as now, I only wished to tour and before I finally sold the Carlton I'd got through innumerable tyres, chains, cassettes and brake blocks, just as I would do with my new Genesis.

I patted the slightly spongy black saddle before addressing it. "I might have to change you for a more traditional leather one," I said, before remembering how long they took to break in. "But not till after we've been to Scotland." I stroked it. "And back," I added, because Simon's tacit challenge was still fresh in my mind. To ride about three hundred miles in a few days on a loaded bike would be quite an achievement, but to repeat the experience after a week's rest would, I felt, validate my status as a bona fide touring cyclist.

I spent at least an hour riding around the estate, stopping often to make adjustments to the rather heavy bike with its relatively wide 32mm tyres. It was wonderfully comfortable to ride, but when I hopped onto my titanium bike to check that the saddle heights tallied I felt like I'd swapped from a carthorse to a thoroughbred. Back on the driveway I patted the highly-strung beast and promised to ride her on my Sunday outings with Simon and co. I then attached the front and rear racks and panniers to the new bike, but refrained from filling them with junk, as I expected my camping gear to arrive the next day. I was about to enter the house to make a coffee when I yelped on realising that I had yet to fit a single bottle cage. After rummaging desperately through the bits of cardboard I found a plain box with the three aluminium cages inside, so I quickly fitted the usual two within the frame. Before loosening the bolts for the super-cool one beneath the down tube, quite close to the chainset, I held the cage in position and decided not to attach it yet. It would look superfluous and rather silly down there, so I put it away for the time being, but after my coffee I nipped back in and screwed it on.

When the parcel courier stepped out of his van at 11.14am I was already waiting by the rear doors, rubbing my hands.

"Expecting a blow-up doll or summat?" said the stout young Prestonian.

I eyed him sternly. "No, some camping gear."

Presently he handed me a large box. "Is it for the grandkids?"

"No, for me, for a long cycle tour."

He whistled through his yellowed teeth. "Rather you than me, mate. See ya."

"Bye," I said. "Yes, go and swill your beer and scoff your pies, you great lummox, and see what state *you* are in thirty years from now," I added sotto voce, before scampering inside with my goodies.

I believe that during the latter years of my working life my sense of self-importance became slightly inflated, because not only was I in charge of a rather large staff, but I usually appeared on the scene like a blustering new commander-in-chief who immediately set about shaking things up and making his weaker troops fear for their posts. After my initial reforming campaign I settled down and I believe that the personnel who remained – usually almost all of them – respected me for my assertive efforts which would, in the long run, make their jobs more secure. Although I didn't really like this rather arrogant side of my character, it had always done the trick, and work was work, after all.

That was all over now and I was just another retiree, but as my cycling fitness improved I gradually detected a fresh flaw in my relationship with my fellow man, that of disdaining all those who had an unhealthy lifestyle. I invariably grimaced on seeing my ex-postie neighbour over the fence, as despite getting fatter by the day he was often to be seen slumped in a wicker chair, snacking in the sun or slurping beer of an evening. The fact that he may have felt that he'd walked quite far enough during his decades spent delivering our post didn't occur to me, and had we not had a rather heated dispute over a borrowed – and subsequently broken – lawnmower some years earlier I might have tried to convince him to get off his arse and do something to conserve his health. Still, when his arteries finally became clogged the NHS would perform a bypass operation and set him on his feet again for a few more years, and only if diabetes struck would he have to reform his dietary habits.

"Live and let live... or die," I muttered as I unpacked my dinky tent and hurried into the garden to try it out. Sarah had already ridiculed my newfound fitness snobbery, pointing out that I too had been a flaccid lump not so long ago and still would be had she and Simon not bullied me into getting back on the bike, so as I wrestled with the springy poles I promised myself to be more tolerant in future. I was one of the lucky ones who had seen the light, and if others courted disease and premature death that was their business.

Twenty minutes later I still had death on my mind, because my one-man tunnel tent felt rather like a coffin from the inside. Its maximum height of 75cm fell to 40cm at my feet and I didn't fancy trying to while away a rainy evening in it. As we'd had so much sunny weather and the forecast promised more I feared that the heavens would surely have to open in the not too distant future. While lying there looking up at the taut nylon I imagined riding all day long in the rain, then having to cook, eat and sleep in that confined space. When Simon and I were conquering our first continent we would of course spur each other on to withstand whatever the weather threw at us, be it scorching deserts, windswept plains, sodden valleys or icy mountains, but on this first tour I'd have to toughen myself up little by little. I grinned on picturing myself taking refuge in a convenient four-star hotel, then groaned on remembering my confounded Cycling Budget.

"Oh, stop worrying about everything," Sarah said shortly after finding me zipped into my sleeping bag inside the tent at half past five. I'd inadvertently nodded off and awoken to find my mind still dwelling on the possible pitfalls of my modest maiden tour, so after expressing my concerns about the Scottish climate I'd grumbled that I'd have to weather every storm because hotels would devastate my budgetary plans.

Sarah sneered. "Forty years ago you'd have taken a little tour like this in your stride, and I don't imagine you had money for hotels then."

I unzipped and crawled out onto the grass. "No, but I could afford you... yes!"

"Me, what?"

"No, you...th hostels. Hostels were cheap as chips and... oh, but will I be allowed to go at my age?"

She laughed. "Of course you will. Ageism isn't allowed these days, though you may have to share a dorm with some high-spirited youngsters."

"If it's peeing down I won't care."

"So are we already in countdown mode?"

"Eh?"

"To the tour. Am I to suffer two whole weeks of increasing anxiety as the fateful day approaches?"

I perused my mental calendar. "More like three weeks, actually."

"How many days are you going to allow for the trip?"

"Three, I think."

Emitting whoops of laughter she entered the house to begin the dinner prep which my untimely snooze had delayed.

Over the tasty pasta she'd rustled up I insisted that my bicycle tour was to be precisely that, a tour spent predominantly in the saddle. As I didn't intend to waste time pottering around villages or lying in fields chewing bits of straw, I'd have at least twelve cycling hours at my disposal each day. "And as I can't possibly average less than ten miles an hour, I'm bound to do at least a hundred miles a day."

"And what if it rains?"

"If it rains, what can I do but soldier on?"

"It seems an awfully long way to ride in three days."

I then played my cunning trump card. "But I simply must keep costs down, love. The fewer nights I'm on the road, the less likely I'll be to cop out and seek expensive lodgings."

She frowned pensively, but I went on to almost ruin my ruse by pretending to ponder on the possibility of a practically non-stop ride.

"Don't talk rubbish, Tom."

"I'm not. Folk have ridden from Land's End to John o' Groats in two days or less, so what's a mere three hundred miles? I'd probably take the odd nap on a convenient bench, but I should still make it in a day and a half. I... I could fill my front panniers with boiled spaghetti and just suck it down whenever I got hungry," I quipped.

She sighed. "You've got this cycling budget business on the brain, so just forget about it for now. Take your time and stay wherever you have to, as I don't want you arriving in Banavie in a state of exhaustion. Kay and Mike like hiking, remember, so we'll be doing plenty of that."

The mention of our outdoorsy, nature-loving, bird-watching holiday companions made my subsequent smile a rather forced one. They liked nothing better than to amble through woods, pointing out every item of flora and fauna that we passed and photographing most of them, but more about them later.

"On Sunday I'll ask Simon how many miles he thinks I should do per day," I said. "Now let's change the subject, as there's more to life than cycling."

She speared an olive. "Yes, there used to be."

On Sunday the sky was overcast and on the exposed road between Pilling and Cockerham the wind assailed us from the south-east. Despite, or because of, my slow rides on the heavy bike I was feeling surprisingly strong and I powered along at the head of our group of six, sticking close to the edge of the road so they couldn't benefit from my slipstream, but being a gutsy bunch of lads they all clung on till I eased off on entering the village. When Frank remonstrated I claimed I was just trying to reach the cafe at Glasson Dock before it rained – which it didn't – but in reality I'd been enjoying my new-found fitness on my most favourable flat terrain.

"Your mindset doesn't seem very touristy," Simon said later on back at Roots Cafe, where he and I usually repaired alone for an end of ride chinwag. I'd had another blast along a short stretch of the A6 on the way back and had managed to detach Mark from the single file behind me.

"Oh, that bit of the old time trial course must have temporarily rewired my brain, ha ha." I then told him about my fortuitous meeting with Bob Taylor, who Simon knew from his short spell of club riding many years ago. "But despite his sexy bike I've resisted the temptation to follow in his tyre tracks, because I'm a committed cycle tourist now."

"Yes, Tom."

"Now, do you think I should ride up to Fort William in three days or four?"

He smiled. "I think you should go for a trial run first."

"I've done that, more than once."

"I mean an out and back ride, with a night of wild camping thrown in to test your mettle."

"Yes, well…"

"Sue's given me the green light for next weekend, so I'll be at yours by nine on Saturday, come rain or shine. We shan't be buying anything en route, so pack everything you need."

"But… but where are we going?"

"Leave that to me."

"But…"

"And afterwards we can discuss your proposed mileage to the Highlands, OK?"

"Yes, Simon."

"And don't spend all week pestering Sarah about it, as she must get some rest of an evening."

"All right."

"And don't fret about it."

"No."

"Because I have your own interests at heart."

"Yes, you usually have."

9

During the next six evenings Sarah plugged her ears every time I attempted to raise the subject of our mystery mini-tour, so on Saturday morning I rolled down our drive ready for anything. I was surprised to see Simon's bike equipped with only two panniers, as opposed to my four plus my rolled tent strapped to the rear rack. I asked him where he intended to sleep.

"Don't worry about that."

"May I lift your bike?"

"If you must." He stepped off and held mine as I lifted his.

"It isn't all that heavy. I hope you aren't planning to rely on my abundant resources."

"No, I'm self-sufficient." He lifted the front end of my bike, then the rear. "Which bag is the kitchen sink in?"

"I'm prepared for every eventuality. This is a trial run, after all."

"Quite right, and you'll see what you really need. Let's go."

We rode to Chipping along the usual quietish route and when the last clouds rolled away I saw that we were in for a very warm day. Simon led the way to the public toilets, where he surprised me by topping up a water bottle of which he'd drunk only about a third.

"What was the point of that?"

"We'll need at least two full bottles the way we're going."

I grinned. "I've got these three and two more in my bags."

He shrugged and pushed off, but only as far as a nearby bench, where he proceeded to sit down.

"What are you doing?"

"Having a rest."

I glanced at my watch. "But we've only done thir... an hour and a bit."

"So what? We're touring. Do you fancy a brew?"

"Not really." I glanced at my watch again.

"Forget the time."

"All right."

"And the miles."

"Eh?"

He laughed. "I know a GPS watch when I see one, Tom, however basic it is."

I instinctively covered my bottom-of-the-range Garmin. "I couldn't help it. I simply have to see my miles as I'm doing them."

"Yes. What's our average?"

"Oh, I dunno."

"Liar."

I sighed. "12.4, but is it such a sin to want to know it?"

"For a tourist, yes, but never mind."

I soon became fidgety on the bench and as the view of the car park was uninspiring Simon agreed to set off. We rode up a fairly demanding hill towards Whitewell, but despite his far lighter bike he lagged behind me, spinning a super-low gear and surveying the scenery far more than he did on our Sunday rides. After whizzing down the other side he spied a prettily situated bench near the sparkling River Hodder and rolled to a halt. This time, a measly five miles after our last stop, he insisted on brewing up, so I made to open the rear pannier containing my cooking gear, but he stayed my hand before extracting a minuscule hob from his pannier and attaching a tiny gas canister to it. He filled a small pan with water from his bottle and before long was able to offer me a plastic mug of coffee with a sprinkling of powdered milk.

"Ta. What about you?"

"I'll make mine now and drink it from the pan." So he repeated the process and all told we spent what seemed like an age on that bench, watching several other cyclists ride past, some hammering away and others pottering along.

"Being such a warm day, we can take our time," Simon said just as I was about to nod off.

"Yes, well, I don't know where we're going, but I can see it won't be very far."

He chuckled as he stood up and stretched. "Come on, let's ride a bit more."

When he pulled up outside a house in the lovely village of Slaidburn just six slow miles later my impatience betrayed me and I told him I simply didn't wish to rest again.

"Keep your hair on." He knocked on the door and asked an elderly lady if she would be kind enough to fill his empty bottle, which she was, so we soon pedalled on down the street, turned left, and began to climb Tatham Fell, a tough six-mile climb with a few downhill respites which I'd last tackled over forty years ago, as it had played no part in my subsequent time trial training schedule. I told Simon that I'd ridden over it on my way to Hawes Youth Hostel when I was about seventeen.

"Then back the next day. Two tough rides, but we took our time." We crested a rise and freewheeled for a while. "Me and my mate Neil would just ride, stop here and there, fool around a bit, and never worry how fast we were going, as we always got there in the end. Yes, this is bringing it all back."

"I'm glad."

"Did you think it would?"

"I suspected it might. We'll think about having some lunch soon."

"There's bound to be a cafe in Bentham."

He just tutted.

After a thoroughly enjoyable descent during which my disc brakes performed well, Simon led me to a bench just off the road before the village, overlooking the pleasant River Wenning, where he allowed me to prepare lunch for us. I pulled out my sturdy single-hob stove, attached one of my two gas canisters, chose the largest pan from my collection of three, then filled it from my abundant water supply. Simon winced on seeing the boil-in-the-bag rice, but as it was such a nice day we didn't mind waiting almost twenty minutes for it to cook, after which I heated up a two-tin mess of beans and stewing steak in another pan. Passing ramblers seemed curious to see two mature men playing house in the midday sun, but the meal was tasty enough, and nicely rounded off with thick slices from one of the two weighty fruitcakes I'd brought along. I made the coffee this time, with real milk, before eyeing the pile of washing up with fear and loathing. Luckily Simon was kind enough to scramble down to the river with my half-full bottle of washing-up liquid and a dishcloth, so I followed soon after with one of my two towels.

Fatigued after our labours we lay down on the grass for a while, but less than two hours after stopping we were back on the road. I assumed we'd be riding into the Yorkshire Dales, so when we took a right a mile or so after Bentham I pointed out that we were heading south again.

"Yes, but only because I have to be home by noon tomorrow, otherwise we'd have gone on to Hawes, just like you did when you were a lad."

"I remember washing plates and myself in streams in my teens. Those fuzzy memories are definitely becoming clearer."

"Yes, all we're lacking is some challenging weather, but you can't have everything. Are you ready for Bowland Knotts on that ever so slightly lighter bike of yours?"

"Yes, I can handle another five-mile climb at this speed. Ah, I suppose it is nice to take our time, but I can't see me doing this all the way to Banavie."

"Why not?"

I shrugged. "I'll want to make headway. Maybe when I get past Glasgow I'll feel like taking it a bit easier." I remembered our holiday companions. "Or a lot easier, as I won't mind arriving a day later than them."

"You'll have to play it by ear. Touring should be about freedom, not schedules. I believe it's best to adapt to circumstances and never plan ahead too much."

"Is that how you mean to go about your continental tours?"

"Definitely. I won't really be *doing* a continent, but spending the two or three months just following my nose. I hope to meet some interesting people in out of the way places and if I think it's worthwhile stopping somewhere for a week, I will. My ideas are still vague, but as the time draws nearer I'll begin to do some research and make my open-ended plans."

"And tell Sue."

"Yes, that too."

After another long and not overly taxing climb over the wild Bowland moors we descended rapidly to a large reservoir, then turned left and arrived at the Gisburn Forest Cafe, situated in a clearing within an extensive fir plantation. Simon told me we were breaking our no-spending rule so that I might check out the agreeable place for future reference. We'd arrived just in time to order coffee and cakes and I noticed that most of the departing customers were rather dusty mountain bikers.

"Yes, there are several mountain bike trails from here. There's a campsite too and some indoor accommodation."

"Really?"

He pointed at a few unmistakably tent-like structures in the field. "Yes, but we have other plans today. I don't suppose you've ever been mountain biking."

"Not properly, no."

"Hmm, I once rode around the intermediate trail here with a friend who was into it. I enjoyed the challenge, but it wasn't something I wanted to pursue, though you might like it."

"I doubt it. I like the feel of tarmac under my tyres."

"Me too, but in a lot of places in the world there are networks of tracks and gravel roads that aren't to be missed, so on my tours I might have to adapt and use a mountain bike, or what they've recently christened gravel bikes, really just modified cyclo-cross bikes, but a great way to get another few thousand quid out of susceptible cyclists."

So we talked bikes until the staff expressed a desire to close and after Simon had topped up his water bottles we went on our way. I'd been hoping he'd hint that I might be welcome to go touring with him, but he didn't. I assumed he was hanging fire until I'd proven myself to be a suitable companion, so I resolved not to moan, groan, whine or whimper, no matter where we ended up spending the night.

As we continued south along a mostly descending lane I pointed out the profile of Pendle Hill in the distance.

"Yes, it's a noble hill and its history of witchcraft makes it seem all the more atmospheric."

"Ha, we could camp on top of it."

"That's what we're going to do."

I wobbled. "Eh?"

"That's to say, not right on top... hmm, but then again, now that we're here." He looked from his shoes to mine, both of the SPD type with recessed cleats. "Damn it, mine have decent soles for walking, but yours are almost smooth. No, we'll have to stick to Plan A."

"Which is?"

"To ride up the Nick of Pendle and camp not far from the road. To get to the summit from near Barley there's a stiff climb up a steep track. Oh, well, another time, perhaps."

We soon rolled to a halt at Sawley and found our best bench of the day, on a grassy bank overlooking a wide bend of the River Ribble. There were a few pub tables nearby and I felt quite intrepid compared to those beer-guzzling loafers – I jest, honestly – but was I adventurous enough to lug my weighty bike up a hill which I had in fact climbed a few years earlier? In the bottom of my left-hand rear pannier there nestled a pair of lightweight pumps, you see, but I wasn't sure if I should disclose their presence to Simon, as one section of the climb had been hellishly steep and consisted of large stone steps up which the bikes would have to be carried. When the sedentary boozers became a bit noisy we rode down the road and strolled around the atmospheric ruins of Sawley Abbey, from where the 'Big End' of Pendle was clearly visible under the still-blue sky.

"Shame about your shoes," Simon said as we padded across the freshly mown grass between the medieval remains.

I gazed up at the hill. Maybe one day he'd want us to wheel our bikes up to Machu Picchu or somewhere, so now was the time to show him that I was up for anything.

I stopped and slapped my forehead lightly. "Oh, I've just remembered. I've brought some pumps, so we can walk up Pendle after all."

He slapped me lightly on the back. "What a terrible actor you are."

"Oh…"

"And I knew you must have more footwear within that mountain of stuff." He rubbed his hands together. "Come on, we may need all the daylight that's left to get there."

About an hour later, after another hard climb from Downham, we reached a gate at the end of a lane some way above Barley. Our day's cycling had ended and now we just had to reach the peak which towered above us. Luckily there was a slightly easier route than the steep stone staircase, up a totally unrideable track, so I huffed and I puffed as I pushed my bike, and though weary after our long day, my disposition remained sunny while the actual sun began to set. Nearing the top we crossed paths with a lone fell runner whose fatigued face and small knapsack suggested that he too had made a day of it. He and I exchanged grins of complicity, I believe, as we both felt the satisfaction granted to those who push themselves to greater heights. Soon we were all alone at the trig point, enjoying the rapidly dimming view.

"You'd better get that tent up quick," Simon said as he pulled two items from his pannier, a compact sleeping bag and a bivvy bag.

"I've brought a good torch. Besides, we still have to make some supper."

"I'll take care of that."

While I erected my tent on a flattish bit with nice springy grass, he busied himself in the light of his head torch and we were soon tucking into vegetable soup and thick corned beef butties. After a cup of tea he slipped into his bags while I sat on my foam mat, enjoying the temperate breeze.

"You'd have had a bad time in that bivvy if it had rained, Simon."

"If rain had been forecast I've have brought a tent, and we wouldn't be up here. We'd be near a village with a pub, in fact, as one must adapt to the elements. There's no point having a rotten time if it can be avoided."

"I'm glad we came up here. It's rounded off the day nicely. Made it complete, so to speak."

I was hoping for some words of approbation, and maybe a hint that we'd tour again sometime soon, but his reply was non-committal – just a gentle snore, in fact – so after a final glance at the star-filled sky I crawled into my tent.

Simon unzipped it at seven and handed me a lightweight trowel.

I yawned. "What the hell's that for?"

"If you wish to go to the bathroom, you'd better do it now before the first walkers arrive."

So I soon stumbled off to find a discreet spot, before adding a trowel to my mental checklist. In the meantime Simon had somehow contrived to fry several rashers of bacon and a couple of eggs in a flimsy frying pan, which we ate with buttered bread. I remarked that he'd certainly optimised his limited luggage and had wanted for nothing.

"I brought just what I knew I'd be using. When you get home and unpack you'll have to think about which things you won't need in a month of Sundays. What tools and spares have you brought?"

"Just about every tool I could possibly need, plus a spare folding tyre, three spare inner tubes, a spare chain, four spare brake pads, a few spare spokes and nipples, four spare cables, insulation tape, duct tape, cable ties, oil, and… I think that's about it."

He laughed. "That's perfect."

"Yes?"

"Yes, for when we go to Outer Mongolia, for instance."

"Ha, right." Despite the chilly morning air I felt the blood rush to my cheeks, so I began to wash the plastic plates as best I could with water from a bottle. While striking camp I decided to take his Mongolia quip with a pinch of salt and refrain from pestering him about his touring plans, because in two years no end of things could happen, and who was to know if I'd really want to go conquering continents?

After struggling down the hill, much to the amusement of a few early-bird walkers, I changed into my cycling shoes and we rode the twenty-five sunny miles home in high spirits. I then bored poor Sarah to tears with a blow-by-blow-by-blow account of my greatest outdoor adventure for over forty years. She eventually made for the French windows with her hands over her ears.

"God, just imagine what you'll be like when you get to Banavie."

"Yes, well, it'll be flora, fauna or my tales of derring-do, so you'll be able to take your pick."

She shuddered. "I think I'll take my violin."

"You do that."

10

Without much more ado I'll move on to the start of my Scottish journey (first leg) because during the next couple of weeks nothing of note happened, except that I disobeyed Simon and planned my trip down to the last detail; several versions of it, in fact, in case it should rain lightly or heavily on days one, two, three or four. Having plenty of free time, I managed to do this surreptitiously, aided by the Tour de France, which the plucky Welshman Geraint Thomas was busy winning in an unobtrusive sort of way. As we had Eurosport I pretended to have spent hours on end in front of the box, whether they were climbing Alps or just whizzing along the flatlands, when in fact I just watched the last few miles before reading a race report in one of the better online cycling magazines.

I was pleased that good old Geraint was winning, of course, and I did enjoy a few of the mountain battles, but I'm a doer rather than a watcher, I told myself, and what I did was to devise my route, with multiple variations, and locate upward of thirty places where I might or might not sleep, ranging from boutique hotels to seemingly suitable spots for wild camping, including a promising bus shelter on the edge of an Ayrshire village. All this meant that my daily mileage, which had to average about eighty, could in fact vary between forty and over a hundred, dependent on meteorological conditions, my physical and psychological state, and possible mechanical issues which might require a diversion to an urban centre, but only if my frame or forks broke, because my abundant tools and spares would cover just about anything else. Simon had urged me to lighten up in this respect, but with Mongolia, Machu Picchu etc. in mind I'd decided to go fully loaded.

So, my departure date was set for Wednesday the first of August, and imagine my surprise when I had not only a dental assistant to see me off, but also a real live dentist. Simon's canines twinkled, then disappeared as he frowned at my bike.

"All those bags are fit to burst."

"Oh, as it's not such a long journey and the forecast is good I thought I might as well test myself a bit."

"I see."

"And carry what I'll need for the longer tours I mean to do."

"Fair enough. Where will you stay tonight?"

I shrugged. "I've no idea. I'll play it by ear and decide this evening. I've got a bivvy bag too, so I can sleep anywhere."

Sarah tittered. "You should see his browsing history on the laptop, Simon. His research has been positively encyclopaedic."

I growled as I bent to adjust a strap, miffed that she'd rumbled me.

"Yes, I knew he'd do a lot. It's human nature really. How do you mean to get past Glasgow?"

I straightened up and grinned. "Glasgow? I won't be going anywhere near it."

"Edinburgh then."

"Ditto."

"He's been looking at ferries," said my nosey wife.

"Good thinking. Well, let's go and fix some teeth while this intrepid man of leisure begins his real bicycling adventures." He shook my hand warmly. "I wish I were coming, Tom. Take care, and don't overdo it today."

"Thanks, mate."

Sarah kissed me, before checking the tightness of my helmet. "Yes, be careful and I hope to see you on Saturday evening, though there's no need to hurry."

I smiled like Ranulph Fiennes heading out to buy the paper. "I'll be there by Saturday all right."

They waved from the driveway as I rolled away, eager to put my familiar roads behind me and blaze a brand new trail. In order to achieve this in the shortest possible time I rode straight up the A6 as far as Garstang, which wasn't too bad because of the frequent stretches of good cycle lane, before taking the quieter road through Cockerham to Lancaster. Once through the busy city I headed to Hest Bank and took my first break – on a bench, of course – overlooking Morecambe Bay. I'd ridden twenty-six miles in a shade over two hours and was feeling like a million dollars. The light wind was favourable, the sky cloudy, and the temperature about eighteen degrees; perfect conditions for a reasonably long first leg which would make the next three days a positive doddle. Yes, if I can manage over a ton today, I mused as I munched a fruit bar, I'll have three seventy-mile days left to do. Ha, seventy miles in a whole day! I'll be able to sit on practically every bench I see, brew up innumerable times, crash out on the grass whenever I feel like it, and get to my destination feeling only slightly fatigued. Thus reassured, I hopped onto the bike and made a beeline for the Lake District.

At this point in the writing process Sarah warned me not to describe every single mile of my route, as it would be a pity if readers who had braved a hundred pages of my cycling apprenticeship finally slapped the book shut on the road between Bolton-le-Sands and Carnforth, for instance, bored to tears by the pedantic account which she'd had to suffer due to the sanctity of our marriage vows. So, although every pedal stroke of that unforgettable first day is still etched on my mind, I'll fast-forward about thirty miles to Kirkstone Pass, which I'd reached by way of Milnthorpe, Crosthwaite and Windermere on a mixture of quiet and busy roads. This famous pass over to Ullswater which climbs for about two and half miles at an average gradient of seven percent was to be my first big test of the day and I found that my mini-tour with Simon had prepared me amply for the challenge. By spinning a low gear and admiring the rugged scenery I crawled up it without undue exertion, sniggering when two lads whizzed past, panting like mad, but of course they weren't going nearly as far as me on their super-light bikes.

At the summit I treated myself to a slap-up lunch at the Kirkstone Pass Inn and as I sipped my coffee in the mild sunshine, gazing down at a sliver of Lake Windermere in the distance, I felt like I really was on top of the world. Here I was, at sixty years of age and after cycling for a little over three months, almost sixty miles from home on a horrendously heavy bike and still feeling as fresh as a daisy! It was a miracle what the human body could endure, mine at least, and with a long downhill stretch ahead I saw no reason why I shouldn't get as far as Carlisle that day. Over a second coffee my mind began to buzz with the possibility of reaching Scotland. I imagined my conversation with Sarah that evening.

"How far did you get, Tom?"

Yawn. *"Oh, in the end I decided to stop in Gretna Green."*

Gasp. *"So far?"*

"Yes, the day turned out so nice that I just kept pottering on. I could've gone further, but I saw no sense in overdoing things."

"So how far have you ridden?"

"Oh, I forgot to look at my watch. About 115 miles, I think, more or less."

"Good heavens!"

"Not so far really." Yawn.

"You sound tired."

"Eh? Oh, no, just a bit sleepy after all that fresh air. I'll probably just do about eighty miles tomorrow, as I can't get into the house until you arrive."

Sigh. *"Are you sure you haven't done too much?"*

Chuckle. "Yes, love, don't worry about me. The bicycle's a tremendously efficient machine, you see, and if you take it easy you can go on forever."

"Phew, I must say I'm impressed."

Modest shrug. "Goodnight, love."

I pushed away my coffee cup, as two always made me hyper, before paying the not inconsiderable bill and pedalling off. My legs felt a tad stiff, probably due to sitting down for so long, but after the long descent I soon got back into my stride and as I rode alongside Ullswater I even had to warn myself to slow down a bit. That hilly 65-mile day with Simon had been my longest ride so far and I'd already exceeded that, but I'd have no Pendle Hill to lug my bike up today, so I pressed happily on, missed my turning, and found myself heading towards Penrith on the busy A66. I could have stopped to consult the map, but as I had Scotland on the brain by then I crossed the bustling market town and headed up the A6, which was surprisingly quiet and wonderfully flat for much of the way.

On approaching Carlisle I sensed a certain weariness in my legs, but as I wasn't far off the hundred mile mark I rode fearlessly through the busy city and after a short refuelling stop on a bench by the River Eden I managed to find the road to Rockcliffe and thence to Greta Green. Those last few flat miles along a road right next to the M6 were hard work, but my sense of achievement was such that I paid little heed to my aching muscles. When I crossed the River Sark into Scotland I whooped for joy, before entering the town and stopping at the first chippy I saw, where I bought two fish, an extra-large portion of chips, and a tub of mushy peas, before devouring them on the nearest bench.

It was then that I made one of the biggest mistakes of my life. With an impressive 111 miles on the clock I should certainly have called it a day and found a room at one of the many B&Bs in the pleasant little town. Had I done so I believe that by resting for a while, then treating myself to a couple of pints and another bite to eat, followed by at least eight hours' sleep and an abundant Scottish breakfast, I could have gone on my way relatively unscathed by my rather excessive first day. I'd have been tired, to be sure, but I believe I'd have managed to put in a few hours on the bike – maybe sixty miles' worth – and still been on track to reach Banavie in four days.

But I didn't do that. After another strong coffee washed down by plenty of water it occurred to me that I still had up to three hours of daylight left. If I rested for another half hour... but no, that might cause my tender legs to shut down for the night, so the best idea would be to set off right away and head towards Dumfries on the quieter roads via Annan. It was only twenty-odd miles, after all, and what a tale I'd have to tell Sarah and Simon, not to mention anybody else who cared to listen! Obviously after this monumental ride I'd be able take it easy for the rest of the trip, so why not achieve a seriously high mileage whilst in an ideal position to do so? I began to imagine another conversation, this time with an astonished and mightily impressed Simon, but I cut it short and heaved my heavy leg over the bike. During the coming days I would often look back on that moment of enervated euphoria... and groan once more at my stupidity.

Yes, the road to Dumfries proved to be the straw that broke the cyclist's back, because before reaching Annan, some ten miles away, I realised that my bum was becoming increasingly numb and my aching feet were revolving in ever-slowing circles. While traversing the small town I half-heartedly looked out for hotel signs, but my mind, vision or both must have been impaired and I soon found myself on the open road once more. Despite the flat terrain I stood up on the pedals frequently, just to ease my aching arse, but each time I sat down I realised that the wear and tear down there was probably not of the kind which could be repaired in a single night.

After unenthusiastically viewing the sea at Cummertrees I vaguely remembered that just up the road in Clarencefield there was a pub with accommodation, so I battled on for four more agonising miles before almost coming to grief on the last climb of the day, the four-inch kerbstone onto the pavement outside the long, low building. After leaning my instrument of torture against the wall I pushed open the door of the Farmers Inn and tottered up to the bar, smiling weakly at the half dozen patrons, who looked ever so comfy in the snug little place. The rosy-faced landlord, I presumed, smiled and waited for me to choose my poison, so I obliged by pointing at the Tennent's pump.

"A pint?"

"Yes, please, and a room for the night," I uttered huskily.

"I'm afraid we're full."

I grasped the bar and flopped onto a stool. "Oh, no..." I whimpered.

He smiled. "Come far?"

"Too far." I looked at my watch, but the figures were hazy. "From Lancashire." I slurped my lager. "Should've stopped sooner."

"It's only ten miles to Dumfries. Plenty of rooms there, even in August."

I shook my head. "Too far. Knackered." Slurp. "Just have to camp."

"You passed a couple of sites near Cummertrees."

I sniffed. "Too far back. Got a bivvy bag. I'll find a spot and jus' sleep."

The man shook his head and walked away. Serves me right, I thought. An overeager teenager riding far too far is one thing, but a mature gent like me… he must think I've got a screw loose and can't wait to get shut of me. No room at the Farmers Inn, so I'll have to find a stable and crash out on the straw…

"There's a room you can use," he said into my left ear. "It's just had a new window fitted and needs decorating, but my wife's making the bed for you now."

I could have hugged him, but I just slumped against the bar, weak with relief. "Thank you, you've… thank you."

He patted me on the back. "Do you want some food first?"

"No, thanks. Fish an' chips in Gretna. Jus' need to get to bed." I took another swig of my beer and pushed the glass away, before stepping off the stool and grasping the bar again, as my legs wanted no more to do with my febrile brain. "I'll go now."

"Er, your bike's outside."

Leave it there, I thought. "Yes," I said.

"I'll wheel it round the back. Go through that door and you'll see number four."

"Thanks."

The plump lady of the house looked aghast at the sweat-stained, bow-legged wretch who peered into the twin room, but she soon rallied and helped me to fetch my bags from the nearby bike. She then ordered me to have a shower, because I'd feel better for it, and told me I could have breakfast as late as nine o'clock.

"Thanks very much. You've both been so kind."

She shook her head and sighed. "You ought to know better at your age. Push bikes are for youngsters."

"Yes, they are. Goodnight."

In the shower I winced as I soaped my nether regions, as the skin had been breached in several places, but there'd be time enough to think about that the next day. Once between the pine-scented sheets I remembered to text Sarah. Using my last ounce of cunning I wrote the following:

In B&B near Carlisle. Good day but tired, so off to sleep now. XXX

That should buy me some time, I thought, before checking the clock. Five to ten. Ten hours' sleep ought to put me straight. Easy day tomorrow. *So* glad I found this place…

11

While wolfing down my delicious Scottish breakfast I tried to convince my matronly hostess that I was almost fully recovered after my epic 127-mile ride.

She shook her head and tutted liberally. "You were at the end of your tether last night, laddie (sic), and you ought to rest today."

"Oh, I'll have to ride a few miles. I'm just a bit concerned about my... about sitting on the saddle," I said, before spearing a lump of black pudding.

On stepping gingerly out of bed an hour earlier I'd realised that although my feet and hands were sore, my legs like jelly, and my back a bit stiff, there was no earthly reason why I couldn't get on my bike and slowly make my way towards Ayr, about seventy miles away. I recalled how I'd belittled that laughably short distance the previous afternoon and immediately began to psych myself up for the day's ordeal, but on going to the loo I realised that my crotch was in a sorry state. The application of some antiseptic cream was a painful affair, but I reasoned that if I later smeared on some vaseline and maybe wore both pairs of padded shorts I might be able to soldier on, just like the Tour de France heroes of yesteryear who had to ride three hundred miles a day and fix their own bikes if they broke down. Would a few light abrasions have stopped them in their tracks? Of course not, and nor would they interrupt my far easier tour.

While finishing my third cup of coffee I told the lady where I was heading. "So I've got three days to do about two hundred miles. I should be able to manage that."

"If you've any sense you'll ride to Dumfries and take the train to Glasgow. Then tomorrow you can ride along the bonnie banks of Loch Lomond and you won't have *too* far to go."

I pictured Simon's smiling face. "Oh, no, I couldn't do that."

"Why not?"

"Well, I have to ride all the way there, don't I?"

"Do you?"

"Yes, that's why I'm doing it."

"And you say your wife's driving up in the car on Saturday?"

"That's right."

She shook her head once again. "Another English eccentric."

"Ah, well, last year a compatriot of yours called Mark Beaumont cycled 18,000 miles around the world, in seventy-nine days."

"Did he now?"

"Yes, and that's well over two-hundred miles a day."

"And how old is he?"

"Er, in his thirties, I think."

She shrugged, smiled, and began to clear the table.

When I was ready to leave, her husband presented me with a modest bill, having charged me half-price due to the scruffy state of the room, so after contributing twenty quid to a local charity I thanked him once again and he stepped outside to see me off. On witnessing my wince as my bum touched the saddle he told me about something a friend of his had done many years earlier while cycling to Cape Wrath.

I laughed. "I doubt it'll come to that, but I'll bear it in mind. Goodbye!"

"Take care now."

After a few hundred excruciating yards I reached the first bend in the road and soon rolled to a halt on a convenient driveway, before dismounting with a plaintive moan. I considered riding the ten miles to Dumfries out of the saddle then calling it a day, as there was no way I could ride much further in my condition. I'd begun to despair when I remembered the remedy the man had mentioned a few moments earlier. His friend had begged an old cushion from a Highland cottager and strapped it to his saddle. I'd been in no pain while eating breakfast, and although I hadn't packed a cushion I did have a foam mat to sleep upon, so it was the work of a few moments to whip it out and fold it until I had a sort of cushion roughly ten inches square and three thick. On realising that it should indeed stop the lacerated bits from coming into contact with the saddle, I dug out my duct tape and soon made a semi-permanent foam sandwich, before lowering my saddle the requisite three inches. After a wobbly false start I realised that in order to propel myself along sitting on such a wide base I'd have to forget about correct positioning and put my saddle down as low as it would go. I also made some double-sided duct tape and affixed my cushion, so that I'd be able to stand up on the pedals without losing it.

On trying my modified bike for size I was delighted to feel only slight discomfort, but on hearing a guffaw I turned to see two blokes observing me from within a compound containing a motley selection of tractors.

"I've got a very sore arse and have to take desperate measures," I called cheerfully.

"Aye, good luck to you, mate," said one, before I gave them the pleasure of seeing me ride off like one of those Victorian cyclists on a prototype bike which should never have left the drawing board. My knees rose high in the air and I couldn't generate much power, but I believe that was partly due to the excesses of the previous day. Still, I was on the road again and, primed for a little ridicule by the gawping tractor men, I either ignored the few tooting drivers I came across or gave them a sunny smile, because failure had been averted and I assumed that my wounds would heal a little and maybe enable me to cut the foam mat the next day and make do with less radical padding.

On joining the extremely busy A75 the tooting intensified, but I soon headed into Dumfries and was surprised to find myself ignored by most pedestrians. I pedalled awkwardly through the town and joined the A76, another fairly busy road, as my original plan of going by way of New Galloway had to be ditched in favour of expediency. The periodic toots continued, but I felt happy to be making ten-mile-an-hour tracks towards Ayr and I chortled to myself from time to time on recalling that Sarah, and therefore Simon, believed I'd begun the day somewhere near Carlisle. Whether or not the truth would come out at some point I didn't care just then, because the landlady's suggestion of catching a train to Glasgow had been an exceedingly tempting one. It would, however, have nullified my modest achievement, and would Mark Beaumont have considered hopped a freight train after one of his painful crashes? Not on your life, as there'd have been no Guinness record after that, and I too felt that my first real tour ought to be an unbroken ride from A to B, and then from B to A because, believe it or not, as I pedalled ridiculously along the mostly flat road I felt more determined than ever to make the return trip too.

Why does one wish to do these things? I asked myself as I ate a snack on a bench in the village of Thornhill, twenty-five miles into my journey (and almost fifty from Carlisle, ha ha.). A few months earlier I'd been a busy hotel manager looking forward to the ease and endless leisure of retirement, and now here I was, perambulating atop a foam cushion through the Scottish Lowlands. I decided that it wasn't the time to philosophise, but I did ponder awhile on what I would have been doing had I not taken up cycling. That grotty shed would already have been repaired, no doubt, and other domestic chores completed. The gardens would be blooming, with weedless beds and impeccable lawns, but how else would I have occupied my time? I'd have walked and read more, and perhaps even resumed the short-story writing I'd dabbled at in my forties, but what on earth would I have written? Tales of suspense set in hotels and/or suburbia? No, all things considered I was glad to be cycling again and after my tour I'd begin to plan the next one. I glanced at my peculiar bike. Or perhaps I'd hang up my panniers for a while and resume my rapid rides on my titanium bike with a view to... no, not racing, but possibly setting myself some speedier kind of challenge. Either way I'd be staying healthy doing something I enjoyed and burning off the excess energy which otherwise might make me restless and irritable.

I set off again, still hoping to make it to Ayr that day, but in my unorthodox riding position I soon began to feel tired, restless and irritable, so after another ten miles I pulled into a rest area by the River Nith. There, seated at a picnic table for a change, I consulted my abundant route notes and elected to check out and hopefully check into the Lochside House Hotel, about sixteen miles up the road. The posh-looking place wouldn't be cheap, but if I threw budgetary caution to the wind and also spent some time in their spa I might be able to speed my recovery and actually enjoy the final two days, touch wood.

I certainly didn't enjoy the final two hours of that day's fifty-mile ride, because my unergonomic position really began to take its toll and I had to stop four more times before reaching my destination, due to sheer tiredness. While lounging on a bench in New Cumnock, just a couple of miles shy of the hotel, I hit upon a solution which might well put an end to my suffering and enable me to complete my journey in a dignified manner, rather than torturing myself for two more days. After slapping my throbbing thighs to celebrate the brilliance of my idea, I remounted and sped down the road with renewed vigour.

"I'd like to stay for two nights," I said to the pretty receptionist.

"Certainly, Sir."

"And use the spa today and tomorrow."

"That can be arranged."

"And... have a massage."

She consulted her screen. "I can fit you in today at five or tomorrow at twelve."

"Er, tomo... no, today, please."

"Very good. How will you be paying, Sir?"

With reluctance, I thought, as this would put a big hole in my cycling budget. "By card."

"OK." She looked me up and down. "Are you on a bicycle?"

"Yes."

"Malcolm here will show you where to store it." She grinned. "We have exercise bikes in the gym, though I don't suppose you'll wish to use them."

"I doubt it."

Half way along the leafy lane to the cluster of modern buildings overlooking a tiny loch I'd removed my cushion and restored the saddle to its correct position, but after a few moments upon it my bum informed me that I was about to make a very wise move. On a place-to-place trip there's no law against having a day off and hopefully the spa waters would help my wounds to heal. I wasn't all that eager to have my muscles pummelled by a stranger, but at the Tour de France and other long races the daily massage is considered essential, so I hoped mine would somehow sort out my poor old legs which didn't know what had hit them.

After a late lunch in the almost empty dining room I rested on my comfy double bed before making my way to the massage parlour, where I was shocked to find a beefy bloke with a grizzled beard awaiting me, rather than the lithe young lady I'd pictured in my mind's eye. The big brute eyed the suntan stripes on my legs.

"A cyclist, eh?"

"Yes."

"Come far?"

"Almost 180 miles in two days."

He slapped a meaty hand on the massage bench. "Shorts and top off."

I complied. "Er, my legs are feeling very delicate."

He grinned down at me as he oiled his hands. "I've helped out at the Tour of Britain a few times, so I know exactly what you need." He frowned. "Hmm, your legs are getting hairy, but I'll manage. Face down and I'll work on your body first."

"Oh, my body's fine."

"Face down."

As I looked through the hole at the top of the bench I gritted my teeth, but his great paws slid smoothly up and down my back and I began to relax. Yes, after a shower and a dip in the spa I'll go to the bar, order a nice cool beer, and call Sarah. I'll tell her the truth about my trip, as she'd get it out of me eventually anyway, then promise to arrive in Banavie on Sunday without fail. Then I'll order a big juicy steak for din… "Aargh!"

"Relax, pal." he said as his hands dug into my poor left calf. "A lot of lactic to get rid of here, so you'll have to grin and bear it."

"Mm."

"If you'd got one of the girls you'd have liked it better."

"Mm."

"But it'd have done you sod all good. Bloody hell, they're tight."

At that moment in time I felt unable to tell him about my two distinct riding positions, but his uncompromising approach appeared to be doing the trick, so when he laid into my thighs I gritted my teeth and bore the pain with fortitude by imagining that I was Geraint Thomas the evening before that final crucial mountain stage of his victorious Tour. On completing his work the not so gentle giant wobbled my thighs from side to side.

"They'll be as good as new tomorrow."

"Thanks, they feel much better. Er, do you know much about saddle sore…ness?"

"Yep. Let's have a look."

As I was putty in this man's hands by then, I pulled aside my boxers, grasped my 'tackle', and cocked my leg.

"Hmm, yes, but it's not too bad. Antiseptic cream, plenty of fresh air, and have a day off if you can."

"I will."

"Then a bit of vaseline and you'll be good to go. Saddle boils are what you have to be wary of. On the Tour of Britain in 2015 there was this Dutch rider with one as big as a bloody egg, so the doctor got this long needle and…

On leaving the massage room I felt a mixture of relief and optimism, because my legs seemed refurbished and the mighty masseur had reassured me that my saddle sores oughtn't to hold me back. I wondered if I'd been a bit of a wimp by copping out and making my silly cushion, thus quite possibly becoming the most photographed cyclist in south-west Scotland that day, as I'd noticed a few smartphones pointing my way, but on recalling the stars I'd seen on mounting the bike outside the Farmers Inn I concluded that innovation had been the better part of valour, if that makes sense. I'd also shown myself, and many others, that I didn't give a hoot what folk thought of the lengths I was prepared to go to in order to complete my tour. I felt, in fact, rather pleased with myself when I called Sarah from the bar terrace before dinner. I managed to condense my stirring saga into a five-minute blow-by-blow account to which she listened in near silence.

"So what do you think of that, love?"

Her near silence continued for a few more moments, before she cleared her throat. "I'm impressed, Tom."

"Impressed? Not, er…embarrassed to be the wife of an eccentric who'll go to any lengths to complete his personal but not especially important challenge?"

"No, just impressed by your stoicism."

I chuckled nervously, waiting for the punchline. "Ha, right."

"I mean it."

"Well, thanks, love, but you didn't see what a sight I must've looked on the bike with that daft cushion and my legs pumping up and down like er…erratic pistons."

"Yes, I did."

I instinctively surveyed the terrace. "Eh?"

She laughed. "While you were nattering on I was looking for you on Instagram. I found you under 'crazy cyclist Scotland'."

"Ah, that explains your rapt attention to my tale. Did I look very silly?"

"Oh, just middlingly silly. Hang on a minute… yes, and anyone who knew anything about cycling would have realised why you were doing it."

"Yes."

"That's what Simon says anyway."

"What?"

"I sent him the photo and he's just replied."

"I see," I said doubtfully, not being all that au fait with this social media business. "Send it to me too then."

"I can't. You want nothing to do with rubbish like Instagram, remember."

"That's true. Anyway, I'll be staying here for two nights. I'm afraid it'll be rather dear, what with the spa and all."

I sensed that she shrugged. "That's all right. Your cycling budget is your own affair."

"I thought you might say that."

She smiled. "But I'll let you off this time, due to your idiotic heroism."

"Thanks, love."

"But don't do it again."

"No, love. Just two seventy-mile days to go."

"OK. Oh, it's going to rain here this weekend."

I gulped. "There?"

"Yes, all over the north of Britain, I'm afraid."

I squeezed my beer glass. "Not to worry. A bit of rain never did anyone any harm. I'll call you on Saturday to tell you how far I've got."

"You do that. Ride carefully."

"I will."

(That lone Instagram photo, by the way, remained on the site for a few weeks then sank without trace. Otherwise I could have contrived to get a copy for the cover of this book, perhaps.)

12

The rest of my stay at the hotel was pleasant, save for one niggling annoyance. The sky remained clear all day Friday, but the fact that Saturday's forecast was awful blunted my enjoyment of the spa, the bar, and the sunshine, because I felt that I should have been on the road, nearing my destination, rather than lazing around like an oriental potentate with a minor attack of the clap, due to a constant urge to scratch my tender spots which I managed to overcome, in public at least. I apologise for failing to put this disagreeable topic to bed, but in bed that night I was still worried that my soreness might jeopardise the rest of my trip, especially if I got soaked through right away.

In the event the rain didn't begin to fall in earnest until I'd reached the outskirts of Irvine, some thirty miles into my so-far tolerable ride. After a short, bleak break by the roadside underneath a large shopping centre I reluctantly donned my rain jacket and braved the elements, determined to reach the ferry terminal at Gourock within three hours. Due to a mostly helpful cross-tailwind I made good progress along the coast on the A78 and the discomfort caused by the rain was assuaged by the fact that my saddle soreness was only slight, a minor miracle considering how bad it had been. After lunch in a twee little cafe in Largs, where I devoured my steak pie and chips as I dripped on the floor, I hit the road again and was delighted when the rain ceased and the sun began to put in an occasional appearance. Modern cycling clothes dry fairly quickly, so I was able to enjoy those last few miles along the coast, with splendid views of the Isle of Bute and the Cowal peninsula, and reached Gourock having ridden sixty miles in only six hours, including stops.

In Gourock and nearby Greenock there are plenty of places to stay and a faint warning bell urged me to call it a day and get some rest, rather than catching the frequent passenger ferry across the Firth of Clyde to Kilcreggan, because on the Rosneath peninsula the hotels were few and mostly expensive. Nevertheless I soon found myself chugging across the estuary on the neat little ferry, as I had about ninety miles left to ride and didn't wish to reach Sarah's side the next day in a state of exhaustion. It was while admiring the views along with the other passengers, several of whom had weighty rucksacks, that I remembered I was fully equipped to camp, had intended to camp, and jolly well ought to camp for at least one night after the wanton self-indulgence of the last two days.

So it was that I rolled down the ramp and along the jetty having resolved to reach Arrochar, at the end of Loch Long, about seventeen miles away. From there it was barely a mile east to the bonnie banks of Loch Lomond, where I'd find campsites galore, but as I pedalled along the almost deserted road I convinced myself to shun the crowds of campers, some of whom might get rowdy on a Saturday night, and bed down alone in the great unknown. For a man who'd camped atop Pendle Hill it ought to be a cinch to find a nice flat spot by the loch and consume some of the food I'd carried for well over two hundred miles. In this way I'd round off my action-packed trip in an intrepid manner, and on my return leg… well, we'd see about that when the time came.

The thought of my forthcoming camp actually made the riding seem easier, because I knew I could stop whenever I wished and wouldn't have to engage in tiresome verbal intercourse with civilians, many of whom failed to understand what drove men like Geraint Thomas, Mark Beaumont, Edmund Hillary and myself to push ourselves to the limit in our quest for… whatever it was, but this spell of conceited reverie carried me all the way along Loch Long until Satan placed temptation before me in the shape of various places of lodging in the idyllic village of Arrochar, nestling between the loch and lovely wooded hills.

Ah, my mobile kingdom for a shower, a slap-up meal, a couple of pints and a comfy bed! But no, if Sir Edmund had lazed around at base camp, feasting on yak meat and being coddled by his Sherpas, who would remember him now? I only wished to impress Sarah and Simon, especially Simon, and to do this I simply had to break my camping duck and become at one with nature for a single night. Having an inkling that the road to Tarbet and Loch Lomond would be busy, I instead rode around the top of Loch Long and found a promising camping spot within some trees quite close to the water. After ineffectually stamping on the lumpy ground I pitched my tent with difficulty, before beginning to prepare my evening meal of stewed steak and beans. Having learnt my lesson back in Bentham with Simon, I eschewed boil-in-the-bag rice for bread and olive oil, as my margarine was looking a bit jaded by then.

I thoroughly enjoyed that meal, sat betwixt the lapping loch and the quiet road, but when it began to rain again I chucked the water I was boiling for my tea, zipped my stuff into the well-concealed tent, and made a beeline back to Arrochar, where I spent three blissful hours sipping first coffee then malt whisky in the Ben Arthur Bothy, a cosy pub with lochside views which I took a peek at occasionally, before wincing and ordering another drink. My bike had lights, of course, so shortly before closing time I rode cautiously back to the tent, crawled into my bag, and was asleep before I could say, 'Thank God I didn't spend the whole evening in this nylon coffin.'

The following day dawned fairly bright, so after breakfasting on a four-egg omelette with bread and olive oil, washed down by lashings of instant coffee, I struck camp, bundled up my soggy tent, made use of my lightweight trowel, then lugged my bike back up to the road, before re-entering the foliage and applying a bit of vaseline, as I still had a long way to go.

"Ah, here you are at last," Sarah said about ten hours later on opening the door of the modern bungalow little more than a stone's throw from the southern end of the Caledonian Canal, that engineering marvel whose final sea lock, or rather loch lock, was to thrill me inordinately during the coming days and remind me that there were far greater feats of human endeavour than piddling cycling trips.

"Yes, here I am, after 72.4 miles along busy but beautiful roads, at an average spee–"

"Spare me the stats for now, Tom. You're filthy." She sniffed. "And you smell."

I shrugged. "I wild camped, but the loch looked a bit cold to bathe in." I grasped her hands. "And I was in a hurry to see you again, my love."

She allowed me to peck her on the cheek. "Get in the shower and I'll bring you some clothes."

"And the wildlife fanatics?"

"Birdwatching somewhere up the loch."

Once I'd donned my clean togs Sarah made me a snack to keep me going until dinner time, then asked me to bring her up to speed regarding the latter part of my trip.

"Well, I… oh, but I'll have to tell Kay and Mike too, so shall I save it for later?"

"No, let me have it now."

"And them?"

She sighed. "They won't be interested in all the gory details of your adventure, Tom. Please don't scratch your crotch."

"Sorry."

"And as you'll have failed to spot a single interesting bird or flower, if I were you I'd just wait for them to ask you about the trip." She handed me a mug of tea and made herself comfortable. "Right, I'm all ears."

Our week in Banavie is largely irrelevant to my cycling-centred account, save to say that we did the usual touristy, outdoorsy things and had a pleasant time, as the weather stayed mostly fine. Our friends were as incurious about my cycling feats as I was regarding the finer points of their nature research, but we got along well and I filled any dull spells with thoughts of my return journey.

One quiet morning after cleaning, checking and oiling the bike, I spread most of the stuff from my panniers on the garage floor and marvelled at the amount of it I'd lugged all that way unnecessarily. I then reattached the rear panniers and began to fill them only with absolutely essential things. Why, for instance, did I really need the tools for removing the cassette? I hadn't snapped a spoke while carrying all that weight and in the unlikely event of breaking a rear one on the drivetrain side I could either tweak the remaining spokes or call in at a local bike shop. The bottom bracket tool seemed even less essential, and did I really need a spare folding tyre?

There and then I decided to throw caution to the wind and ride back to Lancashire with even less tackle than Simon had carried on our mini-tour. Much less, yes, because as I paced around the garage I resolved to complete the return journey in three days, after booking cheap accommodation in advance. I shoved my cooking stuff into the now redundant front panniers and cackled as I folded and stashed my recently aired tent and sleeping bag. Goodbye fully loaded tourer, hello speedy bike! Not so speedy with those heavy tyres though, so I considered sneaking into Fort William to buy some lighter ones, before dismissing the idea because we only had our friends' car and Sarah wouldn't be impressed by such an unnecessary expense, what with me having a far speedier bike back home.

My thoughts then turned to my titanium racer and the sort of rides I'd wish to do after resting up for a few days. Would I content myself with the usual bacon-butty runs and the sociable Sunday outings with Simon's group, or would I need a new kind of challenge? I then pictured my old racing rival Bob Taylor's flashy time trial bike outside the cafe at Chipping, but I shook my head to dispel this disturbing vision. No, to compete in the discipline which had become so irksome to me all those years ago would be a retrograde step which might kill off my new love of cycling. I would become so obsessed with equipment and training that I'd end up bombing around the flatlands, seeing nothing but the road from my aerodynamic position, before poring over the data at home and driving Sarah up the wall.

Besides, racing against the clock on busy roads no longer seemed as true a test as it had in the past. Every time trialist knows that the busier the road, the more the traffic sucks you along, and if a slow lorry happens to dawdle past you stick with it for as long as you can. Some wily exponents of the art of drafting have been known to ride in the middle of the road to allow a lengthy queue to build up behind them, before moving aside to benefit from the subsequent procession of vehicles, caring not a jot about their irresponsible behaviour, so long as they can improve their precious personal bests. Simon had told me that nowadays 'drag-strip' courses have become more prevalent, situated on busy dual-carriageways where the starting point is higher than the finish, and if that's not deluding oneself I don't know what is.

No, what with these factors and the cutting-edge equipment, to call time trials the 'Race of Truth' as we had done – normally when mocking road racers who often trundled around in a bunch before sprinting at the end – no longer seemed valid, so I dismissed the idea of competing in them from my mind. My eyes then alighted on the GPS watch strapped loosely to my handlebars and I found myself grinning. What was to stop me from devising my very own time trial course on the flat, quiet lanes near my home and setting a personal best over ten miles, for instance? That way, whenever I got the urge, I could try to shave off a few seconds and thus get the racing bug out of my system. As I'd only be competing against myself there'd be no need for aero-handlebars or any other go-faster aids, so I'd effectively be using the same sort of bike as I had back in the eighties. I frowned on realising that I'd probably get nowhere near my old speed, but what did that matter? Better to face reality than kid myself like poor old Bob, who lugged his aerodynamic pot belly around drag-strip courses on his state-of-the-art bike week after week, while his wife made arrangements to flee from her fanatical chump of a husband.

Thus my thought process returned to my own lovely wife, whose forbearance mustn't be tested too acutely. I promised myself that after my blistering return journey I'd take it easy for a while and catch up on my domestic chores. Hard training has to be assimilated anyway, so a break would do me good.

"Training?" I said to the saddle which seemed to have finally broken me in. "Is that what I'm doing?"

I shook my head, switched off the lights, and went to join my sensible, multi-faceted companions. After booking my B&Bs for Sunday and Monday I hardly mentioned cycling during the rest of our stay. I didn't even think about it all that much, though I had rather humdrum cycling-related dreams every single night.

13

At this particular point in the writing process Sarah advised me to make more of an effort to describe the scenery I pedalled through, just as her favourite authors would have done. I pointed out that when most of them had been writing there'd been no films or television, and in the case of Jane Austin not even photos, so they'd felt obliged to pen endless descriptions of lush valleys, leafy glades, wooded knolls and whatnot because their city-dwelling readers might never have seen them. I argued that everyone and his dog knew what Scotland looked like, and who was I, a retired hotel manager and born-again cyclist, to attempt to depict scenes that could be viewed on the computer in a jiffy.

"Besides, it isn't that sort of book."

"Suit yourself. Waffle on about your mileage instead then." She feigned a yawn.

"I shall just describe the salient points of my fine achievement, so go and play your violin, as you've a concert next week."

This exchange occurred towards the end of 2020, by which time my cycling career had experienced various ups and downs and a few fairly remarkable things had happened, but when I look back on my three mile-eating days between Banavie and Fulwood I still feel rather pleased with myself. This time there were to be no crippled bums or shattered legs, and although I felt extremely tired on completing each day's ride, after many hours of sleep and copious refuelling I was able to confront the next stage in fairly good shape.

While cycling south along Loch Linnhe at seven o'clock on that sunny Sunday morning I did feel a certain sense of trepidation, but it was great to be on the road again after a week of sightseeing, strolling, eating, drinking and, above all, lots of chatter. Before my cycling comeback it would have seemed like a perfectly satisfactory holiday and a welcome break from work, but once I'd recovered from my trials I'd begun to feel increasingly fidgety and purposeless. This fragmentary approach to leisure time – doing a bit of this and a bit of that until each day is finally over – would have been my ongoing fate had it not been for cycling, and as I began to climb into the hills beyond Loch Leven I reflected that setting oneself the task of riding about 115 miles before sundown was a wonderful way to concentrate the mind.

By this time I certainly didn't share Émile Zola's experience of thinking about nothing whilst cycling, because during a long and not overly strenuous day in the saddle I found myself pondering on all sorts of things – from Sarah's music through tumbledown sheds to future cycling objectives – and only on reaching a town, village or significant junction did I assess my progress and pay attention to my bodily needs, principally eating and drinking. On my first couple of dozen outings I'd thought almost exclusively about the ride itself, but now the bike was beginning to feel like a remarkably efficient extension of my body which carried me effortlessly along, partly thanks to my much reduced load.

The countryside had been lovely before reaching the Trossachs, but beyond the small village of Crianlarich, where I stopped for lunch, the dense woodland skirting the verdant peaks created the 'chocolate box' scenery which brings folk to Scotland in their droves, many of whom seemed to be sharing my road, but the presence of a white line about a yard from the edge gave me a sense of security, especially while being passed by yet another caravan. I could cross the line if I sensed from the tone of a car's engine that the driver considered intrepid touring cyclists to be a nuisance as he – generally a he – hurried back to his stressful life south of the border after lazing around for a fortnight, I invariably assumed, because an active caravanner, who I presumed must exist, would have been more empathic and respectful. Still, I was used to traffic by then and didn't let it bother me too much as I rode alongside Loch Lomond, but it was still a relief to reach Tarbet, as I knew from experience that the bulk of the vehicles would be heading south towards Glasgow.

In Arrochar, after about seventy miles in a little over seven hours, I decided to stop for a second slightly lighter lunch in the Ben Arthur Bothy, that welcome refuge from the rain on the last evening of my first leg. One cheerful waitress remarked that I was looking in far better shape this time.

"Thank you."

"I guess you're being more sensible and doing less miles."

"Oh, seventy down and about forty-five to go, you know," I said, striving and probably failing to remove any signs of smugness from my grin.

She tittered. "Crazy guy."

"Oh, I'm well-rested and my bike's lighter and the weather's much better," I said, fearing that these words would be wasted on the pale, chubby lass.

"I go jogging sometimes, but oh, it's such hard work."

My eyes lit up, I believe, and I asked her to sit down for a moment, before delivering a hasty homily about the advantages of cycling over jogging. I told her that as running was a weight-bearing means of locomotion it took at least a year of assiduous practice before it became in any way pleasurable, while cycling could be fun practically from the word go. "I've only been doing it for a few months and here I am, cycling miles and miles every day. If you can get out for an hour a couple of times a week you'll be flying along in no time, and the road by the loch is ever so quiet."

She gazed at me doubtfully. "But does it burn a lot of calories? That's the main reason I go jogging, to be honest."

I beamed. "*Loads* of calories, because you can cycle far further than you can run. On these trips I'm eating all day long, but I burn it all off." I pictured a typical jogger of her proportions. "I bet you jog along for half an hour and hate most of it."

"Less time, and I hate every minute of it."

"Ah, and I'm afraid you'll only burn two or three hundred calories after all that effort. An hour on the bike will burn a lot more and you'll have enjoyed it and spent more quality time in the country."

She nodded solemnly. "My friend's got a bike and I could borrow my brother's. Maybe we'll give it a go soon."

I nodded vigorously. "Yes, yes, you do that. You won't regret it, I promise you." I inadvertently flexed my bulging thigh muscles. "It's changed my life, I can tell you that."

She smiled. "I still think you're a bit crazy, riding that far at... oh, can I get you anything else?"

I grinned. "At my age? Ha, you'd be surprised what the human body is capable of." I was about to launch into another sermon about something or other when duty called the charming girl away, but when I pressed on alongside Loch Long my mind was abuzz with new and previously unsuspected resolutions. I'd enjoyed hearing the sound of my own encouraging voice so much that I resolved to find a way to hear it more often and thereby help a few people to discover the joys of cycling and end their sedentary ways. By the time I approached the ferry terminal at Kilcreggan I'd decided to consult Simon's wife Sue on the matter. She'd already encouraged me to lend a hand in her charitable work, but I'd have to be adamant that my efforts must be cycling related, or before I knew it she'd have me minding a till in a charity shop two afternoons a week or something similarly sedentary and uninspiring.

I believe this brand-new selfless sense of purpose enabled me to complete the last twenty-odd miles from Gouroch to Ardrossan without suffering excessively, and on stopping the clock after 117 miles I felt a whole lot better than I had after my first really long ride. As I ate a copious dinner at a pub near the B&B I felt that I'd broken the back of the journey, despite still having two more hundred-milers to do. By then

I'd learnt to pace myself, you see, and after riding slowly up each hill I'd coast down the other side without turning the pedals a single time. In a way the flat sections were hardest, as I sometimes had to hold myself back, but during my many short stops I'd stretch and pace around a little before relaxing for a few minutes on a bench or the grass.

Perceptive readers may have noticed that I appear to be retracing my route rather than exploring new roads, and although I knew this to be unadventurous I excused my failing due to the high daily mileage. On my second day's ride to Gretna Green I rode 102 miles in a whopping twelve hours, taking it so easy and stopping so often that I began to fear that once back on my titanium bike I wouldn't wish to push myself as I had done before.

And what of it? I thought that evening as I gorged on takeaway pasta and pizza in the breakfast room of the pleasant B&B. Given my remarkable ability to ride almost half as many miles a day as that steely Scot Mark Beaumont had done on his round-the-world trip – on a speedy bike and with a support crew, I might add – oughtn't I to tackle some kind of distance challenge of my own, rather than burning around the lanes and increasing the risk of getting hooked on racing again?

The most popular long-distance cycling route in Britain has always been Land's End to John o' Groats, about 875 miles on cyclable but often busy roads, and although it would be a great challenge to do it in… a certain number of days, it wasn't a very original idea. I could always extend the trip to a thousand miles and thus avoid the more congested routes, but it would be a hassle to get myself to one end of the country then back home from the other, solely in order to join the ranks of thousands of LEJOG conquerors. As I munched my seventh slice of pizza, however, the idea of riding a thousand miles in… a certain number of days began to take root in my mind and I wondered where I could head to from home which would entail cycling that distance. If I'd had my laptop I'd have prised it open and feverishly begun to plot possible routes all over Europe, but it was too fiddly a task on a smartphone, so my thoughts turned to the timing of my challenge and the likelihood of Sarah wishing to meet me at the other end. She still had at least a fortnight of spare holidays, as a trip to visit an old friend in Cyprus had been postponed due to certain family issues, so might my dear wife fancy flying somewhere, scraping me up off the tarmac, then nursing me by the beach for a week or so?

She might, I thought as I heaved my stuffed stomach up the stairs to my room, but then again she might not. If someone else could be persuaded to join us, ideally Sue and Simon, the trip might be more appealing to her, but how could I really justify a thousand-mile epic ride during the same summer as my epic 2×320-odd mile one? She'd probably become cheesed off by my obsessive pedalling, unless…

"Goodnight," said an elderly fellow who was about to enter his room.

"Ha!" I cried. "Sorry, I've just had an idea. Goodnight," I added, before scurrying into my room and grabbing my phone. My idea was so perfect – self-sacrificing and self-serving in equal measure – that I decided to put it into writing right away, but to whom should I address my textual commitment to this onerous challenge? Were I to write to Sue she'd consider my words binding and I'd struggle to get out of it should I experience a sharp attack of cold feet on the morrow, whereas Sarah would probably just tell me to concentrate on getting myself home in one piece rather than making a promise I'd probably end up breaking, knowing me. After debating between the sheets for a while I decided to write to neither of them, before tapping out my message.

Hi, Simon. Return trip going well so far. I've decided to do a 1000-mile ride in the not too distant future. I'd like to raise some money for Sue's charity. Do you fancy joining me on this worthy challenge? Tom.

That should hit the spot, I thought as I sniggered softly and turned out the light.

The third and final day proved to be the toughest, as I ended up riding 111 miles into a cross-headwind with a few showers thrown in to test my mettle to the limit. Retracing my initial route from Gretna Green took me fourteen hours and during the final stretch along the A6 I was nearing the end of my tether, but Simon's message still buoyed me up, as it had done all day long.

Charity ride great idea, Tom. I'll be with you all the way. Have mentioned it to Sue and she's delighted. See you soon, he'd written while I'd been devouring my last Scottish breakfast for a while.

Great. See you tomorrow evening, I'd replied.

OK. Our hotel in Húsavík is down by the port. I'll get them to boil a sheep's head just for you, he'd responded, his witty way of stressing that life went on without me, in Iceland in their case.

Still, this would give us all a little time to reflect on my proposal, I thought on stopping at the end of our cul-de-sac to wipe my sweaty face and suck down my last energy gel – sugar-laden treats reserved for the final miles of each ride – because I wished to appear slightly less knackered than I felt.

"You look absolutely knackered," Sarah said as I stood erectly by my bike.

"Oh, just slightly fatigued."

She chuckled and gave me a kiss before opening the garage door and relieving me of my faithful, filthy tourer, which hadn't missed a beat during the whole ride.

"Get those clothes off and I'll run you a bath."

"I'll have a shower. I might fall asleep in the bath," I admitted. "Have, er… Sue and Simon been in touch lately?"

"Today."

"Ah, good. Are they having a good time up there?"

"Yes, and I want to hear nothing about your latest scheme for the time being."

"Oh, that. Well, I–"

"Nothing at all until you've come down from you cycling high." She escorted me into the house and shoved me towards the stairs. "You're becoming bow-legged, you know."

"I'll do some walking this week." I grasped the bannister and prepared myself for the final climb of the day. "Just tell me if you approve of my idea, in general terms."

"Yes, in general terms, and so does Sue, as you'll see when you go to her office next Monday."

I frowned. "Her office?"

She grinned. "Charitable endeavours such as the one you suggest are like business propositions to a shrewd lady like Sue and need to be discussed in an appropriate environment."

"But..."

"And I'll say no more on the subject. Would you like some lasagne for supper?"

"Yes, a lot, please."

14

After eating, sleeping and lazing about like a healthy hog for the next two days I began to take a few leg-straightening strolls and catch up with my domestic chores, even re-felting the shed roof in a slightly cack-handed manner, but I hoped it would keep the rain off the mower and the gardening tools which I got around to using later in the week. I had four whole days off the bike, before going for an easy thirty-mile ride on Sunday. Once the old legs had got going my titanium racer felt super-light and fast and it crossed my mind that someone might be willing to drive a support vehicle on my thousand-mile ride, not to follow my every pedal stroke, which would be overkill even on such an important challenge that would probably raise tens of thousands for Sue's charity, but to be there when I needed it and enable me to carry hardly any luggage at all.

By then I'd decided that it was the mileage that mattered, rather than where I rode to, and I'd already traced a not quite out-and-back route from home which would take me as far north as Thurso, but not John o' Groats, as that might cause folk to ask me why I hadn't done the usual prosaic pilgrimage from Land's End like everybody else. The roads in Scotland have to be among the best and quietest in Britain, after all, and I was looking forward to putting my proposal to Sue the next day, before badgering Simon to lay down his dental pliers for a week and join me. Yes, if he came the ladies might well wish to drive the support vehicle – probably my roomy Skoda for which I'd buy a sleek bike-specific roof rack – and an enjoyably arduous and thoroughly worthwhile time would be had by all, before we returned home to watch the money mount up on one of those websites which folk now use when raising funds for charity, Sarah had told me.

The premises of Sue's charity were located on the ground floor of a scruffy house on a shabby street not far from Preston train station. Several rough, unhealthy looking people were hanging around outside, some smoking roll-up cigarettes, while one especially weathered bloke of about forty subtly concealed his can of strong lager as I made purposefully for the door. Inside I found a communal room containing more tough-looking customers, most of whom were sipping coffee and seeming thoroughly at ease, while a couple of them were perusing antiquated computer screens. There were only three women among Sue's fifteen or so patrons and the boldest looking of them asked me if I was after the boss.

"Yes, I've come to see Sue," I said, feeling decidedly uncomfortable in this unfamiliar environment which made a hotel bar full of football supporters resemble a royal garden party.

She pointed a nicotine-stained finger at me. "You got summat to do wi' cycling?"

"Er, yes, that's right."

Her husky laugh revealed an incomplete set of yellow-brown teeth. "You'll not get me on a fucking bike, mate."

I grinned. "No... I mean, you never know."

"No fucking way, dude."

"Well..."

"Go outside if you want to swear, Cath," said a familiar voice from behind me.

"Soz, Sue." She patted my arm. "Want a brew?"

"Er..."

"We'll both have coffee," said Sue, looking very businesslike in a light-blue trouser suit and with her long brown hair tied tightly back. "Come in, Tom."

I stepped into her makeshift office whose shelves were of the metallic, warehouse type, before taking a seat by her cluttered desk. "So this is where you hang out."

"Yes, I know it's a mess, but it's all we can afford, as there's practically no funding at the moment."

"Right. What are all those people doing?"

"They're supposed to be searching for jobs, but as we've only got two computers they have to take turns. Most of them just come for coffee and company really, as they're not very employable. Not yet, anyway."

"So are they drug addicts and... things?"

"Recovering drug addicts and alcoholics, prison leavers, homeless folk, and others who've fallen through the net."

"The net?"

"The net of the welfare state which the Tories are doing their best to undermine."

"Yes, well, I've always believed that folk ought to fight their own battles, generally speaking."

She smiled. "I know. That's why this is going to be such an eye-opener for you, Tom."

I was about to protest that I'd only come to discuss my altruistic thousand-mile bike ride, whereby I could help these unfortunate souls from afar, when Cath came in with two mugs of coffee.

"Cath, Tom here has come to get you on your bikes."

As she put down the mugs her thin white arms quivered. "Fu... not me, he's not."

"Suit yourself, but those who take part will be able to spend time in the country, getting some fresh air and having lunch in a cafe."

Her red-rimmed brown eyes lit up. "For free?"

"Yes, for free, but we've only got eight bikes, so not everyone can go. Not at first, anyway. Tell the others that."

"Will do." She scurried out.

"What's all this about?" I said.

She grinned. "You heard. I've managed to scrounge eight bikes from other charities and I mean to make use of them before the summer's over. My initial plan was just to get them out cycling a bit, but your idea of a sponsored ride has opened my eyes to the great potential of such a thing."

I shook my head. "How on earth are any of them going to ride a thousand miles?" I sipped my coffee. "Ugh! There must be about three sugars in this."

She tittered. "At least. Cath just assumes that everyone wants it. It's cheap calories, after all." She sighed. "Cath was born in a small village, but she came to Preston years ago and got mixed up with the wrong crowd. She's like a... compendium of everything that can go wrong in a young woman's life when they lack a guiding hand. Pregnancy, domestic abuse, alcohol, drugs, prostitution, prison, rehab, roughly in that order. She's got a heart of gold and I really want her to come with us on the rides."

I sucked my teeth. "Us?"

She smiled. "You'll be the group leader and I'll make them behave. We'll try to get out twice a week and build up to a sponsored ride which I hope will raise loads of money. They'll be the key players, but anyone will be able to take part, so you'll have to think of a nice route over a suitable distance."

"Not a thousand miles then?"

"No, not quite, but a challenging distance for them."

"A hundred?"

She almost sprayed me with coffee. "Be realistic, Tom. I was thinking more like twenty, but I'd prefer it to be a bit more if you think they can handle it."

"Look, Sue, I–"

"I'd like us to do it around mid-September, so you've got little over a month to train them up. I think they'd enjoy riding through Blackpool, so maybe you could devise a route which will take us to Fleetwood on quiet roads, then along the seafront all the way to Lytham, then back on quiet roads. Do you think you can manage that?"

I sipped my sickly brew and pondered awhile, then shook my head firmly. "Nope."

"Nope, as in you want nothing to do with us?"

"Nope, nope as in a coastal route would be too far and too busy for much of the way. I suggest a ride to Scorton, out through Inglewhite and back through Inskip. I've done it several times and it's about thirty-two mostly flat miles from Fulwood, so a bit further from here."

"Oh, it's far too busy to ride out of Preston from here. I don't want fatalities on our first ride, even if they are surplus to society's requirements."

"I didn't suggest they were. I'm just not used to being around that kind of folk."

"I know, and as you've offered to take on the challenge you're going to get to know them a whole lot better."

I cursed myself for suggesting the Scorton ride, then found myself slowly coming around to the idea of helping Sue out for a month or so, culminating in an event which ought to raise a lot of much-needed cash for her noble cause. After that I could gracefully retire to my self-indulgent suburban life, satisfied that I'd done my bit for the long-suffering underclasses. Besides, I was in no great hurry to do my thousand-mile ride, and surely Sue would let Simon come with me after I'd earned such a huge stash of brownie points.

"Do you have a minibus at your disposal, Sue?"

She laughed. "I wish. If I did I'd take them out of this grim town every week. Most of them hardly know the countryside at all, you know. They live their lives in their crummy neighbourhoods and the furthest they get is here and the dole office, apart from the ones who've done time. I'm sorting out some bus passes with the council though, so they'll have no trouble getting to Fulwood."

I gulped. "Fulwood?"

"Yes, Fulwood."

"The Fulwood where we live?"

"Is there another? Yes, I've got it all worked out. You and I each store four of the bikes, then their riders come to get them and we meet up at ours, before heading for the lanes just like you and Simon do."

I pictured Cath and a few of the others wandering up my cul-de-sac, before hearing the sound of police sirens. "But what will the neighbours think?"

"Fuck the neighbours, as Cath would say."

I gasped, never having heard Sue say anything worse than bloody before.

"We've both got plenty of room in our garages, but I would like you to check all the bikes first, as I'm not sure when they were last ridden. The charity can afford a few new tyres and things, if they're really necessary."

"Yes, I don't mind servicing the bikes," I mumbled.

"But you don't wish to receive my people at your house."

"No, not really."

She tutted jauntily. "You're still prejudiced, but never mind. What we'll do is this. I'll get all the bikes to your house, then as you service them you can bring them to ours, where our rides will begin. How does that sound?"

"Better, yes, and your garage is massive. Oh, hang on though. What about Simon's precious collection?"

"What about it?"

"Well, those bikes are worth thousands, aren't they? If your people see them, one might take it into his head to go back one dark night and help himself."

She frowned. "Don't be preposterous, Tom. I'd trust all of them with... a lot. They're not born criminals, you know, and when they've nicked stuff it's usually been to pay for drugs."

"Oh, well, that's reassuring."

"Besides, the one or two who might possibly consider such a dastardly deed are still on probation, so they wouldn't dare."

"Yes, well, I'd get Simon to move most of his bikes up to that spare room, if I were you, just in case."

"He wouldn't dare." She shook her head. "You don't understand these people yet, Tom. Look, you could take... Cath, for example, into your home as a lodger and it wouldn't occur to her to steal anything in a million years. In this game it's all about mutual respect, and so far none of them have let me down, not like that, anyway."

"How then?"

She shrugged. "They sometimes fall off the wagon or go back on drugs, but that's only to be expected."

"One guy was drinking beer outside."

"Snitch, but that would be Gav, so it doesn't matter."

"Why not?"

"Because heroin was his real problem. Now he's off methadone too, so I don't begrudge him a drop of drink, as he's done very well."

I pictured eight riders pedalling along in a line, each with a can of Special Brew in their bottle cage. "You will be coming on every ride, won't you?"

She smiled. "Yes, don't worry, you just have to concentrate on the cycling side of things. They must get fit enough to complete the sponsored ride, as we stand to gain a lot of money from it."

"All right." Then I remembered something from my long career. "Hey, come to think of it I've had a few ex-cons working at the hotels, usually in the kitchen. I didn't have all that much to do with them, but most of them were fine."

"Most of them?"

"Yes, one chap got fed up of being bullied by the chef and ended up chasing him around with a big knife, though he swore he didn't really intend to stab him. I managed to hush it up, but he had to go." I straightened my back. "So, you see, Sue, I do have some knowledge of… ruffians and suchlike."

"Hmm, yes, and your hotel experience could come in handy."

"Er, how?"

"Well, you might be able to help one or two of them to get jobs."

"How?"

"Well, if you think they'd make the grade you could give them a reference, for instance."

"That would be dishonest, Sue."

"Yes, well, never mind about that for now." She consulted her diary. "How about if I have the bikes driven round to yours tomorrow afternoon? I assume you'll want to go cycling in the morning."

"Yes, all right." I eyed her shrewdly. "I assume Sarah knows all about this."

"Yes, it's partly her idea."

"I might have guessed. And Simon? What does he think?"

"Oh, he says he'll be with us all the way."

I remembered his first text from Iceland. "Yes, he's fond of using that handily ambiguous phrase."

"He'll be coming on the sponsored ride, and so will his cycling buddies, and they're all going to get lots of sponsors, just like you."

I sighed. "Yes, I expect we'll all end up sponsoring each other. That's usually the way."

"Yes. Right, there's no time to lose, so let's do our first ride this Friday."

"All right."

"Now, one essential enticement to get them to come is the offer of a free lunch in a nice cafe. Simon says there's a good one called Roots not too far away, so we'll go there on Friday. Why are you scowling?"

"Eh? Oh, well, you know, that's my favourite cafe, where I'm beginning to get a bit of cycling cred, but I don't suppose that matters."

"No, because you'll soon have even better cred as a tireless worker for the underprivileged."

I straightened up again, having got into the habit of slouching since stepping up my mileage, Sarah had told me more than once. "I don't know about tireless, Sue. I'm getting my head around taking part in this project, but when it's over I think I'll step back and resume my normal life."

"That's what you say now."

"And I mean it."

"But you may find that this kind of work grows on you. Besides, you won't want to cycle all that much in winter."

I pictured the super-duper turbo trainer I had my eye on. "Don't bet on it."

On the way home I dropped in at a bike shop and bought a dozen brake cables, as my cycling team's machines ought to have at least one brand new one. Later on – and I'll refrain from reporting yet another lengthy chat – I chided Sarah for getting me into something which promised to stretch my comfort zone further than ever before.

"In the end you'll find it rewarding," she said. "You can put your management skills to good use and I'm sure you'll find those people no more troublesome than hotel employees, or not much. There's more to life than just cycling, and you'll still be cycling, so chin up and face this new challenge in the right spirit."

"Yes, love."

"And afterwards we'll talk about your supported thousand-mile ride."

"*Yes*, love."

15

The eight bikes were driven round in a big old van and I was slightly disappointed when I saw the state of them. I enjoy fettling bikes and had been looking forward to finally putting my vast selection of tools through their paces, but the four cheap road bikes, two mountain bikes, and two lightish hybrids with straight handlebars were all in pretty good nick, including the eight front brake cables which I changed anyway, just to be on the safe side. After checking each bike I took it out for a spin and fine-tuned the gears by the roadside, so any vigilant neighbours probably thought I was setting up a clandestine bike shop in my garage. A Trek mountain bike was the best of the lot, having quite expensive components, but it also sported huge knobbly tyres which would slow its rider down too much, so after adjusting the saddle to my height I rode it to the nearest and friendliest bike shop where I intended to equip it with a faster pair of tyres.

I was happy to shell out such a modest sum, but on entering the tidy establishment I wondered what Sue would have done in my place. She never tired of squeezing unwanted goods and even cash out of folk, especially us, for the benefit of 'her people', so as I already knew the friendly owner I asked him if he'd swap the rather upmarket tyres for a pair of cheap slicks, in aid of a good cause. Not only was he happy to do this, as he'd soon find a new owner for the fat tyres, but he agreed to sponsor our ride and advertise it if I gave him some leaflets. After thanking him profusely I seized the moment and asked for a small selection of inner tubes, which I'd stash in my panniers so that none of my team could become stranded on the lanes. He waved away the proffered twenty-pound note, promised to help me out if I encountered any mechanical difficulties I couldn't resolve, and wished me the best of luck, so I grabbed the bike and headed for the door.

"Er, we'd better change those tyres," he said.

"Ah, yes, or shall I do it and bring you the big ones?"

In a jiffy he'd clamped the bike to a stand and had the tyres and tubes changed within five minutes, so I rode speedily home on the slicks, feeling thoroughly pleased with my work so far.

"You know, I'd prefer to form part of the backroom staff really," I told Sarah later. "I think I'd rather fettle a hundred bikes than go cycling with that motley crew."

"Embrace the challenge, Tom."

"Yes, love."

"And by the time you come to prepare your thousand-mile ride you'll know how to get lots of sponsors."

"Er, I thought I might skip the sponsors on that one and just do it."

She tutted slowly, several times. "Oh, no, you'll not get Sue and me traipsing all round the country just for the good of your health. We'll need our motivation too. So, who are you going to get to sponsor you for the Scorton ride?"

"Oh, just the usual victims, I expect."

She grinned. "Simon and me will be badgering our patients, in the chair if necessary, so something similar has occurred to me that you could do." She then told me what it was.

"Oh, no, no, no, I don't think so. Besides, if I just turn up empty-handed their contributions will be grudging or non-existent."

"Sue will have the leaflets ready by tomorrow afternoon, so you can ride up on Thursday if you want to get it over with."

"Isn't she getting ahead of herself?"

"Why?"

"Well, our first ride could be a disaster. They might... disperse with their bikes, never to be seen again."

"Sue knows her people, Tom, and if she says that eight of them will ride to Scorton and back on Saturday the fifteenth of September, you can be sure they will."

"So soon?"

"So soon. She needs that sponsorship money badly, to pay the rent for one thing, so you'd better be a good coach."

I covered my face with my hands. "Oh, gawd, what have I let myself in for? I wish I hadn't retired now."

"You might not say that on Thursday."

She was right about that, because when I rolled to a halt outside my former hotel after a twenty-five-mile ride only marred by the heavy traffic between Lancaster and Morecambe I felt extremely reluctant to pass through the sliding doors, and not just because I was wearing my cycling gear. I'd smiled on seeing the big, ugly edifice, but hearing the swish of the doors reminded me of the thousands of times I'd walked through those or similar doors during the last forty years, usually to face a series of irksome problems which I'd have to resolve before they swished shut behind me. My career had been a constant grind and most of my successes ephemeral, mainly due to the grasping nature of the faceless owners, as hotel chains only care about making money for their shareholders. I was just a pawn in a profitable game and I'm glad to be out of it, I thought as I carried my titanium bike over the polished floor. I noticed the cleaner had neglected to mop the usual dimly lit corner containing an artificial willow tree, so I decided to park my bike there.

Heather, the best of the receptionists, greeted me warmly and we repaired to the coffee machine in the breakfast-serving nook. After complimenting me on my new slimline look, as I'd dipped below thirteen stone at last, she told me that Naomi, the new manager who I'd called the previous day, regretted being too busy to see me, but hoped I'd get plenty of sponsors for my worthy cause.

"Right, is she really busy?"

Heather shrugged. "She's fond of meetings, but my guess is that she doesn't want to cramp your style. She's not very popular at the moment, as she's quite tough on the slackers, and since Andy left the other week she's been feeling a bit stressed."

I sipped my coffee. "I shan't trespass on her new domain for long. These leaflets have the link to our challenge on a fundraising site, so I won't need to try to prise fivers out of folk."

She took one. "Well, I'll be sponsoring you." She looked me up and down. "Don't you feel a bit daft in that get-up?"

"Oh, I'm used to it by now." I told her briefly about my Scotland trip and couldn't resist mentioning my mileage.

"Wow, that's such a long way. I never imagined you doing anything like that, Tom."

I shrugged modestly and muttered something about having a lot of time on my hands.

"Did you not fancy golf in the end then? It sounds easier and a lot more sociable to me."

"Yes, well, I've realised that I'm not such a social animal after all." I tossed my cardboard cup into the familiar bin and noticed the lid needed cleaning. "Right, I'm going to do the rounds one last time."

"Come and see me before you go. I've got some news too."

"Will do."

I went to the kitchen first and felt quite gratified by that motley crew's response to my arrival, as they seemed genuinely pleased to see me. After laughing at my lycra they asked me how I was doing, grumbled a bit about the new boss, and promised to sponsor me if I completed the arduous thirty-two mile ride. I then sought out Dorothy, the head housekeeper, who was ensconced in her den full of washing machines as usual. Her staff, mostly young Polish women who spoke poor English despite having been in the country for some time, were busy doing the rooms, so I handed her a few leaflets and went to find Jim the maintenance man, who was ensconced in his little den full of tools and smelling slightly of cigarette smoke, as usual. Jim was over sixty and an inveterate grumbler, so it was amusing to hear him sing my praises and insist that I'd been a positive angel compared to the sour-faced southern bint – his words, not mine – who wouldn't just let him get on with maintaining *his* hotel as he'd done for over twenty years.

"I must say you do take pride in your work, Jim."

"Yeah, and she'll be here today and gone tomorrow, not giving a toss about the place really."

I smiled. "Like me?"

"No, you weren't one of these go-getters who only think about themselves."

I pictured the photos of the Raffles Hotel in Singapore which I'd once printed out, many years ago. "No, I guess I wasn't."

He scowled at the web address on the leaflet, before handing me a tenner, so I was off the mark even before our first training ride.

"Thanks, Jim. If the ride doesn't come off for whatever reason, I'll post the money back to you."

"Why wouldn't it come off?"

I described the kind of folk who were doing it and mentioned my role in their preparation.

He scratched his stubbly chin. "I reckon if they finish that first cafe ride in a good mood they'll end up doing the sponsored ride. You want to weed out any moaners straight away and get someone else."

"I'll bear that in mind. Any thoughts of retiring, Jim?"

"Nah, not me." He patted his dusty work bench. "I like it here, despite her upstairs."

Back in the reception area I chatted to a few more former colleagues, then followed Heather outside with my bike. She told me that due to an unexpected inheritance left by a defunct uncle in Hull, she and her IT technician husband were going to buy a bed and breakfast establishment in the Cumbrian hills just outside the boundaries of the Lake District. He would continue to work from home, while she'd be able to employ her hospitality skills without having to answer to anyone.

"That sounds brilliant, Heather." I looked up at the red-brick walls. "I sometimes wish I'd done my own thing, but I've still got my health, so it's worked out all right for me."

She smiled and patted the saddle. "And your new hobby. I hope you'll come to stay with us soon after we open next spring. You'll be my guest, of course."

After recalling my temporarily shelved itinerary, I grinned. "No, because there'll be four of us. Two thoroughly knackered cyclists and our wives." I told her about the thousand-mile ride whose penultimate leg would now probably end at her future B&B.

"It's amazing to think that you can ride so far at… be careful in the traffic, Tom."

I grinned. "At my age?"

"Yes. I honestly didn't think sixty-year-olds could cycle so far. I certainly don't know any who could do it, except you, of course."

"Oh, there are thousands of people around the world still doing great feats of endurance at my age or older. Folk run marathons at eighty, ninety and even a hundred. It's principally a mental battle, because the human body is capable of so much more than we think."

I believe she stifled a yawn, so I refrained from spouting any more banalities, gave her a hug, and hit the road.

I chose not to ride back by way of Cockerham, so only on leaving Galgate was I able to relax somewhat as the A6 widened. After negotiating a large roundabout I found myself flying along, partly due to a slightly downhill gradient and a light tailwind, but when the road levelled I continued to pound the pedals and saw – on my GPS watch strapped to the handlebars – that I was exceeding twenty miles an hour, so I did my damnedest to keep that magical figure on the screen for as long as possible. As I powered along with my hands on the drops it gradually dawned on me why I was making this unpremeditated effort. I was on the old Brock ten-mile time trial course, where I'd pulverised myself for twenty-odd minutes on countless Saturday afternoons for several years! Knowing that my trials would be over just before the next set of traffic lights, I strove to adopt an even more aerodynamic position and began to go absolutely flat out. On one easy bit I topped twenty-four miles an hour, but by the time I crossed a familiar faint line on the road my pace had dropped and I was pretty much done in.

I coasted to a halt, communed with my handlebars until I got my breath back, then cursed myself for not having restarted my watch at the roundabout and clocked those five blistering miles. I estimated, perhaps optimistically, that I'd averaged about twenty-two miles an hour, which if kept up for twice the distance would give me a ten-mile time of about… twenty-seven minutes, not all that bad for a spontaneous effort, considering that my best ever time was a little over twenty-two-and-a-half minutes, on a perfect day at the height of my career. I then pictured roly-poly Bob Taylor on his super-bike, before mentally removing him from it and placing myself in the saddle. What sort of speed would I be capable of achieving on an aero-beast like that? Surely a couple of miles an hour faster, I believed, if I wore a high-tech skin-suit and even one of those nifty teardrop helmets I'd seen on the time-trial stages of the Tour de France.

Then, when a gust of wind hit the back of my sweaty neck, I had a depressing thought. Just how strong had that tailwind been? There was only one way to find out, so after having a drink and spending a few moments psyching myself up, I turned around in the road and headed back towards Galgate, steadily building up to my maximum sustainable speed which, alas, didn't exceed nineteen miles an hour and I doubt I could have kept that up for the whole five miles. I soon eased off and turned south again, pedalling easily to allow my brain to make fresh calculations. If truth be told I'd be hard-pushed to do the ten-mile course in half an hour, a measly twenty miles an hour and a positive joke of a time for a man of my middlingly good pedigree. A bike like Bob's might shave a minute or two off… but no, I'd feel like a right pillock doing such slow times atop several grand's worth of equipment. I rode the final fifteen miles home in a distinctly gloomy state of mind, but at least it took said mind off the very different challenge which awaited me the following day.

Over our beef casserole that evening Sarah noticed my melancholy state and tried to buck me up, having assumed that my forthcoming coaching debut was getting me down. I elected to confess to my foolish time-trial tribulations and told her more or less what I've just told you, expecting her to play the same old slightly scratched record about the danger of falling back into my obsessive ways and endangering my blossoming love of cycling. Instead she said something like this.

"First of all, forget your old personal bests. Erase them from your mind, as they're irrelevant. I think you should also forget about that time-trial course for now, because if you don't I can see you traipsing up the A6 on every single ride, then traipsing back down it feeling disappointed with your effort. Instead of doing a nice variety of rides along all the lovely lanes, you'll become a stubborn automaton riding in heavy traffic all the time, a very stupid thing to do. No, if you *must* challenge yourself in that way – and to be honest I don't really see the point – you should measure a pleasant circuit on the lanes, maybe four or five miles long, so whenever you get the urge to ride like a man possessed you can do the loop flat out, then carry on with your ride. If you do that about once a week I think you'll see your time come down little by little and hopefully it'll be enough to scratch that particular itch."

I shook my head in wonder. "Sarah, you should be coaching Sue's team, not me."

"No thanks."

"You know, I think you've hit the nail right on the head. If I am ever going to get fast again that's by far the best way to do it, and I've never had a circuit like that before, so it'll be something new. Yes, a fresh challenge for a born-again speed merchant, or aspiring speed merchant, as I'll probably get to a point where I say enough's enough and turn my attention back to endurance riding." As I mopped up some gravy my lips took a downward turn.

"What's up now?"

"But what if I do get addicted to speed and end up wanting to emulate poor Bob Taylor?"

"We'll cross that bridge when we come to it."

"Yes."

"Or close it."

"Yes."

She patted my hand. "You've done all that before, Tom. You're far better off pursuing new challenges."

"Yes."

She grinned. "What time are you meeting at Sue and Simon's tomorrow?"

"Oh, God." I straightened up. "The fun will commence at ten o'clock."

She rubbed her hands together. "Oh, goodie. I'm sure a fine time will be had by all."

16

"I think it's going pretty well so far, don't you?" Sue said as we approached our goal at midday. The sun was shining but dark clouds populated my mind, as it had been one hell of a job to get our singular squad so near to our destination and I feared that my cycling cred was about to crumble to dust in the patio of Roots Cafe.

I glanced back over my shoulder. "Well, we've covered six whole miles and all seven of them are still within sight."

She smiled. "Ha, just watch how the others fight for that eighth bike now."

"Are you sure? I mean, they've done nothing but complain so far, apart from Cath."

"Oh, it's just their way of dealing with an unfamiliar situation. You'll see how they cheer up when they tuck into their food."

"Hmm." I glanced at my watch and chuckled grimly. "It's taken us almost an hour to get this far."

"I'm sure all cycling teams have their teething troubles."

"True," I said, wondering how Dave Brailsford of the Sky cycling team would go about getting his famous marginal gains out of this lot.

I'd arrived at Sue's raring to go, but only Cath was there, wobbling along the tree-lined avenue on one of the straight-handlebar bikes, as she hadn't cycled since she was a kid and needed to relearn the art of staying upright. In her scruffy denim shorts her thin white legs looked terribly feeble, but I could see she was determined to give it her best shot, so I rolled up the wide driveway of the large detached house feeling quite sanguine about our venture. Then, shortly after ten, the others began to arrive in ones and twos, complaining about the frigging bus or the bloody long walk from the stop or the humid weather, among other things. The first arrivals pounced on the newest and most colourful bikes, regardless of their size, and refused to relinquish them when I tried to redistribute them according to height. That morning I'd told myself to treat them just like a new batch of kitchen assistants, in a firm but good-humoured way, but once amongst that gang of slightly scary misfits my resolve crumbled and I began to dither; always fatal, Sue told me after she'd peremptorily assigned the bikes and ordered them to stand still and stop moaning while I adjusted the saddle height of each one. Then she brought out the brand-new helmets and a similar process began all over again.

Once their precious heads were protected I clapped and led the way onto the avenue, only to find myself alone, as someone needed the loo, another was peckish and two more were thirsty, as we'd neglected to buy bottles for their bikes, an understandable oversight, I thought, given the shortness of our maiden ride. After Sue had smilingly catered to their needs, seeming happy to let them into the house unsupervised, we finally snaked away towards the lanes, riding up to four-abreast at times, but the perplexed drivers refrained from tooting their horns, I was amused to see. After stopping just before the lane commenced I insisted on single-file for the time being, until their dubious bike-handling skills improved, then Sue led the way slowly towards the cafe, but not for long, because a tough young delinquent called Ryan sped away, bobbing up and down in a most unergonomic manner.

"Why's he doing that?" I asked her.

"Oh, he's just been inside for three months, so he relishes his freedom."

"He'll get lost."

"No, he likes the safety of the group too much."

"Make your mind up."

She sighed. "If you'd been in prison you'd understand. You'd better bring up the rear and encourage any stragglers."

So I slowed right down, as Sue's blistering pace – about eight miles an hour – had already made mincemeat of our mini-peloton. Most of them were scowling at the road and/or swearing at the superbly tuned gears which they slammed up or down seemingly at random, but the last rider was grinning as she doggedly pressed the pedals.

"How's it going, Cath?"

"It's fucking brilliant. Haven't been in the country for ages. It smells lovely."

"Yes, it does."

"Though I could murder a fag. Looks like I'm the weakling here. Can't see how I'm gonna do thirty miles in a month's time."

I beamed at the plucky lass. "Oh, you'll do it all right. You've got the right attitude, unlike mos... some of the others."

"Oh, the blokes are right moaning gits, but they like it really. Shame about Gav though."

"Why didn't he come?"

"He did, to the bus stop, then he said he needed a drink and buggered off."

"Oh, dear. Is he so addicted to it?"

"I don't think so. I reckon he just bottled it."

"So we'll have to find someone else for the eighth bike."

"Nah, I'll make him come... next time. This is just what he needs... I'll tell him."

"You do that."

As she was out of breath I dropped back to let her get on with it. On a long straight I surveyed our fragmented crew as they bobbed, weaved, grunted, cursed and spat, while Sue led them serenely along without a care in the world, because by then young Ryan was back in the fold, having enjoyed his taste of freedom for long enough. At this point any especially socially conscious readers may be looking forward to an in-depth account of my involvement with Sue's people, wherein I describe each one of them and delve into their difficult lives, but if I don't depict our cycling squad in great detail it isn't because I didn't value them as individuals, but due to the fact that this account is mainly about my cycling career, not my good works, which may not interest many fellow pedallers greatly.

So within two miles of the cafe things were going fairly well, until a curve in the lane caused a tubby young bloke called John to ride obliquely into a hedge. As he'd been second in line at the time the others laughed derisively – in a rather exaggerated way, I thought – apart from Cath, who helped him up and coaxed him back onto the road after plucking a couple of twigs from his helmet. He'd just lost concentration, he said, which wasn't surprising considering his history of mild mental illness and a serious reliance on antidepressants and whatever else the doctors had prescribed him over the years. Slightly shaken but unbowed, he led the way for a while until Sue's rather worn rear tyre sustained a puncture.

This caused further scenes of merriment, for some reason, but enabled me to increase my kudos by changing the inner tube for one that I had in my pannier almost as quickly as the bike shop owner had done. Sue told them how lucky they were to have such a professional mechanic at their disposal, before pushing off and immediately applying the brakes because a skinny chap called Wayne cried out that he had to take a shit.

"We've only a mile to go," I said to the writhing fellow.

"Gotta go right now, bud."

So, as there were no handy gaps in the hedge, Sue issued a sharp command and within a minute we'd ditched our bikes and formed a human shield around the crouching chap. This show of unexpected solidarity carried out without a single snide comment or peal of laughter surprised me, and when we moved off yet again I told Sue that her people remained a great mystery to me.

"So childish for no good reason, then they suddenly pull together like that." I murmured. "What will they be like at the cafe?"

"Oh, I expect they'll chuck their food at each other and swear their heads off, due to the sheer novelty of it all, but we must just grin and bear it."

"Oh… dear."

It was at this point when she said it was going pretty well so far, but it was with a feeling of great trepidation that I led the way round to the patio, where about a dozen cyclists and as many civilians were quietly enjoying their lunch. While our team were leaning their bikes on the wall or just dumping them on the grass, an elderly couple sporting expensive cameras hastily swallowed the last of their coffee and made for the gate, so six members of our squad swamped that particular picnic table and began to bay for grub, causing a trio of cyclists from Chorley to vacate the adjacent table. Those three were of the well-heeled type who possessed bikes far too expensive for their modest cycling needs, so their hurried exit didn't distress me too much, but I knew most of the remaining riders by sight and prepared myself to become a pariah, because one just doesn't bring a rabble like ours, in their unsporty clothes and already rolling and lighting cigarettes, to a place reserved for civilised outdoorsy types. As Cath puffed greedily on her lung-cleansing fag I lamented the fact that Sue had suggested that we visit Roots three more times before the sponsored ride, as well as instructing me to locate another similar cafe for our Tuesday outings. When John the hedge invader brusquely called over the friendly waitress I made myself small by Sue's side and hoped for the best.

I needn't have worried, or not much, because Sue stood up and called for silence, before taking the proffered menus and handing them out. She also took a couple of sheets from the waitress's pad and told her she'd be in presently to place our order.

"Now, team," she announced. "We can afford to spend about ten pounds per head, including drinks, so please bear that in mind. If you're thirsty after our gruelling ride, order tea rather than coffee, as you get more in the pot and it's more refreshing."

"I want beer," said Wayne, him of the dodgy stomach.

"Unfortunately these premises aren't licenced, otherwise we'd all have whisky and cokes. (General laughter.) So, make your choices and I'll jot them down."

While they were quietly deliberating Sue murmured that they would never squander their dole money on a cafe meal, so this really was a special treat for them, and I must say that from then on their behaviour was close to exemplary and their eating habits far more refined than I'd expected. That last phrase makes me sound like an awful snob, but in my defence I can only reiterate that I'd never mixed with such people before; people who would go on to impress me repeatedly before September 15th, and once again on the great day itself.

Towards the end of the meal the subject of the eighth bike came up and was sombrely debated. On the plus side this meant that the seven nearby bikes had been definitively claimed for the duration, but three of the team opined that

Gav had squandered his chance and should cede his place to someone else. Cath then argued that once she'd told him how pleasant the ride and the cafe had been he would regret having bottled it and wish to come. The sceptics agreed to gauge Gav's response to his reprieve and if he seemed eager to join the team, so be it, as no-one else was desperate to take part, except a youngster called Luke, but he had a pending court appearance which didn't bode well for his future liberty, so there was no point getting him out on the bike if he was to be slammed up a fortnight later, as that would be a right frigging downer for him, said Ryan, who knew what he was talking about.

When Cath whipped out her cigarette papers Sue told her that all being well we'd be back at the house within forty-five minutes. There we would drink more tea in the garden and she could puff away to her heart's content, so the smokers – just six of the seven – agreed to conserve their lung power for the return leg. On the way back I remembered that I was the coach, so I spent a little time chatting to each of them and giving a few tips regarding optimal gearing, posture, hand positioning and suchlike, while making a mental note of a few saddles which needed to be pushed up or down a bit. They all seemed receptive to my advice and most said they were finding the first ride surprisingly easy, so I was able to slip in a few short homilies about the wonderful efficiency of the bicycle and the joys of the open road, but I refrained from pointing out the mental health benefits of cycling, feeling sure that they'd have heard all that before from the health professionals who then stuffed them full of pills, according to Sue.

We arrived at the house without incident and were soon sprawling all over the ample rear lawn, sipping tea, not smoking all that much, and reflecting on our ride. They all agreed that I could up the distance by about half on our next outing, as long as I provided them with bottles, and young Ryan declared that to do the Scorton ride right away would be a piece of piss.

"Yes, love, but not for everyone," said Sue. "And it's not all about that anyway. It's about getting out and enjoying every ride. I know I'm looking forward to them."

A wiry, tattooed chap of about fifty called Colin asked her if they'd get to keep the bikes after the sponsored ride, his cheek causing a short bout of merriment.

"Well, the bikes are ours and are there to be used," said Sue. "But if anyone wants one to use all the time we'll have to look into finding another and coming to some arrangement. Tom, are there many second-hand bikes on eBay for a reasonable price?"

As I barely bothered browsing bikes that cost less than two grand I said I'd have to check. "But I imagine fairly decent ones can be had for a hundred quid or so, if I shop around."

Sue smiled. "Then we'll see who's still keen after Scorton."

Until then none of them had stepped inside the garage, as Sue had prudently wheeled all the team's bikes out before their arrival, but before they dispersed she invited them to take a peek at her husband's collection. An ominous (I thought) hush fell as they gazed with admiration and tentatively stroked the saddles. Ryan inspected each of the eleven bikes so carefully that I wondered if he was calculating their value on the black market.

"Why's he need so many of them?" said Colin.

Sue smiled. "He doesn't, but they all form part of his cycling history, so he likes to keep them."

"Mine's one of them," I said. "Which he gave me to encourage me to take up cycling again."

"I bet he's got a fu… smart car too," said John.

"A Vauxhall Astra," I said. "Bikes are his thing."

"I wish I had my own bike," said Mark, the most 'normal' looking of the team and by far the quietest. "If I get that warehouse job I'll be able to buy one soon, but I won't get it because I can't get there at six in the morning… without a bike."

Sue patted his arm. "You'll be able to use the one you're riding until you get paid."

"Then I'll find you a good one on eBay," I found myself saying, because the thought of the shy young fellow setting this fine example to the others gave me such a thrill that I'd have gladly bought him a bike out of my precious cycling budget on the spot. There were all sorts of reasons why none of them worked, but after we'd seen them off and returned to the garden I pointed out to Sue that anyone who could ride a reasonable distance on a bicycle should also be able to hold down a straightforward job. She opined that when Brexit finally happened a lot of Europeans might return home, so her people would have a far better chance than at present.

"Why take a risk on someone with problems when you can employ a strapping young foreigner who'll work like a demon and take all the overtime that's offered? No, our people have been up against it for a long time now."

"Though I expect some of them don't really want to work."

"Yes, well, they've got out of the habit."

So we spent a while debating how best to motivate our team not to shy away from any work opportunities which might come their way, until I remembered that after Scorton I'd be withdrawing gracefully from the fray and returning to my wholly bourgeois life.

I believe Sue noticed the gleam go out of my eyes. "You may find that these people grow on you, Tom."

I shrugged. "Maybe, but do you really like them – as individuals, I mean – or is this just a noble crusade you're on?"

"Oh, I like them all right. I find them far more interesting than the friends we've known for donkey's years, apart from you and Sarah."

"Why?"

"Oh, I think it's because they're all involved in some kind of struggle. Us lot, well, we're coming to the end of our moderate struggle to become comfortably off, so all that's left are twenty or thirty years of trying to entertain ourselves until we die. I'm finding our dinner parties increasingly dull, but when I mention my work our friends' eyes tend to glaze over." She shrugged. "Still, each to their own. I've got this, you and Simon have your cycling, Sarah has her music, so we're not as aimless as most folk."

"No, I suppose we aren't."

"Damn it. I meant to kidnap Cath and take her to the surgery."

"What for?"

"Simon wants to pull all her teeth out."

"Right. Any particular reason?"

"To give her false ones, of course. She's up for it, in theory, as she knows new teeth will improve her appearance no end, but she's scared of the dentist's chair which she's avoided for so long. Oh, well, maybe on Tuesday you can persuade her it's for the best."

"Me?"

"Yes. You're a man, after all, so if you subtly point out how much they'll improve her looks she might see reason and come quietly."

"I'll try."

After discussing certain aspects of our future rides I rode home feeling that my day of negligible training had been rewarding in other ways. Then I spotted Sarah's dusty bike in the corner of the garage and cackled softly.

"Look," I said a few hours later.

"Yes, you've cleaned it."

"And removed that silly basket and serviced it thoroughly, so you're good to go."

"Where?"

"Wherever you want, but I assume you'll show solidarity and do the sponsored ride with the rest of us."

"Oh, I don't enjoy cycling all that much."

"You used to like pottering along the lanes from time to time. Besides, all music and little exercise makes Sarah...

not overweight, perish the thought, but a tad flaccid, just like I used to be, or so you often told me." I pinched the back of her arm. "We don't want to be getting bingo wings now, do we, love?"

She nodded solemnly. "All right, I'll come out with you tomorrow."

"Good, er... with me?"

She pinched my well-defined right tricep. "Yes, I'll need just as much encouragement as Sue's people, you know."

"But what about *my* training?"

She shrugged. "Fill your panniers with bricks or ride with your brakes on, but to get me out you'll have to come too."

"I'll never become a born-again speed merchant at this rate," I moaned, before casting a longing look at my titanium bike and switching off the light.

17

In the event, after riding an enjoyable fourteen miles with my wife, including a quick coffee at Roots, I swapped bikes and headed off alone to establish a suitable circuit for my private time trials. I started the clock at the top of the motorway bridge just before Swillbrook, not far from the cafe, and headed north-west to Inskip, before riding south-west through Wharles and hoping the five miles would be up before I reached that other motorway bridge I mentioned earlier in the book. Alas, I had to climb that previously dreaded slope and coast down the other side before I could stop the clock, but my inverted V-shaped course ended slightly lower down than it began, so I couldn't grumble. I'd done it fairly briskly and averaged about eighteen miles an hour, so I decided to potter back along some narrow lanes to the starting point and try to set a seriously fast time which I'd attempt to beat the following week. On slowly approaching the first motorway bridge again I breathed deeply and steeled myself for the ordeal I was about to subject myself to, my first full-on effort since my very last time trial at the age of twenty-seven, after which I'd hung up my bikes and later sold them.

"Here goes," I said as I started the clock and stamped on the pedals, intending to make the most of my launch pad. When the wide, well-surfaced lane flattened out I was flying along and a mile later I was still keeping my speed above twenty-three miles an hour, but my lungs were fit to burst and I remembered just how excruciatingly hard time trials were meant to be. I'd started off too fast, of course, and during the second mile my poor old legs were screaming, figuratively speaking, but just like Roger Bannister on the Iffley Road track back in 1954 I dug deep and did my damnedest to maintain my speed. Then, on approaching a left turn where I knew I'd have to look out for oncoming traffic, a funny thing happened. Forced to slow down a little, when I accelerated along the Inskip road I reached a certain speed and decided that it was jolly well fast enough for a keen but mature gentleman like myself. I was still going hard, but I allowed the pain in my thighs to subside to a bearable level and, ignoring my watch, concentrated on maintaining a fluid riding style. On turning left again I knew I'd completed about half the ride and considered digging deeper once I whizzed through Wharles with about a mile to go, but on traversing the hamlet I grinned and even giggled a little, because I felt like a rather clever man. I did push hard up the motorway bridge, remaining seated and still on the large chainring, then I gathered speed down the other side before stopping the clock after five miles, puffing hard but by no means at the end of my tether.

As I pottered homeward, spinning the pedals easily, I reflected on my time of 14.54 and felt pleased to have topped twenty miles an hour without having crucified myself on the bike. I could have gone a bit faster, I knew, but my prudence had put me in such a good mood that when I walked into the kitchen Sarah assumed that I must have exceeded all my expectation, so smug was my grin.

"You look pleased with yourself," she said warily.

"Eh? Oh, yes, I did a fastish five miles." I clicked the kettle on. "Tea?"

"Do I get all the stats now or later?"

"Sergey Bubka."

"What?"

"I'm going to be like Sergey Bubka. Remember him?"

"Yes, but don't you think you're a bit old to take up pole vaulting?"

"Ha, yes, but no, I don't mean that. Do you remember how he kept breaking his own world record?"

"Vaguely."

"I think he spent about ten years shaving centimetres off it one by one. He made more money that way, I expect, and enjoyed the limelight."

"I'm confused."

"Don't you see? He could probably have jumped a lot higher earlier, but then where would he have been?"

She looked into my eyes. "Have you overtaxed yourself, Tom?"

While making the tea I explained my cunning plan to gradually shave seconds off my newly-established five-mile mark without putting myself through hell every time I attempted it. She agreed that this sounded like a sensible idea, but failed to understand why I felt so chuffed about my rather commonplace idea.

I tapped my sweaty head. "I think it's just the way my brain works. I want to have that ongoing challenge, but I don't want to get stressed about it, and nor do I want to kid myself that I'll ever be really fast, as I was never that quick back in the day." I planted a kiss on her forehead. "And the circuit was your idea, so thanks again for that, love. Yes, we should all strive to lead well-balanced lives, but each activity in that life should be well-balanced too."

"Hear, hear, dear. You should set up shop as a cycling psychologist. Bob Taylor could be your first patient."

"Ah, poor Bob, but if that's what makes him happy, who are we to judge? No, Simon's the true cycling psychologist. I'll see what he says tomorrow about my eminently sensible approach to scratching my speed itch."

"You do that."

The following overcast morning as we pedalled along the pleasant B-road between Clapham and Bentham, Simon agreed that my five-mile test sounded like just the job to keep more dangerous demons at bay.

"Like what?"

"You wanna put that route on Strava, Tom," said Frank from behind us. "Then we can all have a bash at it."

Simon groaned. "He's said it. As you haven't mentioned Strava I assumed you were still living without it."

"Yes, well, I don't really want to spend money on a fancy bike computer right now."

Frank rode up alongside me. "You can link up to Strava with just about any GPS watch, even that one."

"Get back, Frank," Simon snapped, doubly annoyed because he hated riding three-abreast even for a few moments. "Well, now you know, so I expect that before long you'll be chasing segment times like so many others."

"Oh, I don't know."

"And if you do put your five-mile route on Strava, the fast lads will pulverise your time and you'll no longer value your own gradual improvements. Oh, well, I suppose it was inevitable that you'd get it eventually, but please don't bore me with your Strava battles, because I'm not interested."

"But you use it, don't you?"

"Yes, but mainly to see my rides on the map." He smiled. "I've done most of my routes many times, but it's still nice to see a big loop like today's. When I start doing some serious touring it'll be good to be able to look back on my progress across Europe or wherever."

"I think a segment starts about here," said Frank from behind us.

"I don't doubt it. Do you remember how Dave used to have kittens every time we dawdled through a promising segment, Frank?"

"Yeah, poor sod. He's just started building a bungalow out towards Longton."

Simon sighed. "I doubt we'll see him out on the bike again."

I twigged that Dave must be the builder who had become so obsessed with Strava segments that he'd resumed his work in order to end his addiction. "I shan't bother with it yet then, as I know what I'm like."

"Oh, I meant to say, the weekend after that sponsored ride that you've roped us into, I'd like to ride to Barnard Castle and back."

"Right. How far's that?"

"Oh, eighty-odd miles each way. I'll probably ride out through Hawes and come back through Leyburn and Kettlewell."

My mouth began to water. "Sounds good. Some nice roads that we never get to from home."

"Yes, and I know a good B&B in Barnard Castle, so just say the word and I'll book us a twin room."

"I'm up for it."

"Good. We'll travel light and hope we get good weather. I thought it would be a nice way to round off the summer months."

"And something to look forward to."

As our ride was a fairly long one we stopped at a cafe in Bentham and I expected Simon to mention the Barnard Castle expedition to the others, as Frank and Mark had probably overheard his comments, but as he didn't I assumed it was to be an exclusive two-man trip, which suited me fine as I always liked to spend some quality time with my friend. I didn't suspect that in the intervening month he would make a momentous decision which would end up affecting both our lives significantly, but more about that later.

I clocked seventy-seven miles that day and arrived home feeling content and only moderately tired. Long rides were what I liked best, I reflected, before wondering how often I'd bother to hammer myself on my five-mile route. I took a look at Strava on the laptop and considered linking my GPS watch to it, but decided to resist the temptation for the time being. When I wasn't out with Sue's people, Simon's posse, or Sarah I'd probably feel like doing some good long rides rather than bombing around like a wannabe racer whose heart wasn't really in it. I suppose I'd been lucky that the first mature time trialist I'd made contact with had been Bob Taylor – still not his real name – because had it been a lean, lithe powerhouse of a man I might have felt compelled to emulate him. The fact is, I told Sarah and myself over supper, that racing is really for relative youngsters who can hope to improve with each coming year, not for oldsters like me, who ought to see cycling as a means to keeping fit and seeing new places.

"Yes, Tom, and I already know about the Barnard Castle weekend, so you don't have to ask permission."

"Ah, good."

"And as for racing, don't make such a big deal of it. Have a go if you feel like it. You might enjoy it."

"Too expensive."

"How absurd. You've got a perfectly good racing bike. Anyway, it's up to you whether you change your car any time soon or squander the money on cycling gear. We only live once, after all."

"That's true." I recalled how much my legs had hurt and my lungs burnt during the second mile of the previous day's time trial. "But I'll carry on as I am for now."

"As you wish."

On Tuesday morning, however, I found myself in a funny sort of race, because after I'd broached a certain subject with Cath she pedalled away at a tremendous rate and we ended up distancing the others.

"You know it's for the best, Cath," I yelled as I watched her skinny legs whizzing round.

"Leave me alone, Tom. There's nowt wrong wi' mi teeth."

"Yes, there is and you know it."

She eased off a bit. "When the next one falls out I'll do it."

I rode up alongside her. "Why put it off till then? Simon's a great dentist and you'll hardly feel a thing."

"They say dentures hurt for ages."

"Don't be soft."

"And till I get them, what? I'll have to keep my gob shut all the time."

"No bad thing."

"Cheeky git."

"Look, if you're tough enough to do this, surely you can bear a bit of discomfort that'll improve your looks so much."

"Oh, I'm no oil painting."

"Not now you aren't." I decided to risk incurring her wrath by trying to be honest. "When I first saw you I thought, oh, she's not a bad looking lass, but when I saw your teeth it was a shock. Such a pity, I thought, then when Sue told me Simon was going to pull them out I felt really pleased. I know the whole process will be a bit unpleasant, but just picture yourself with new teeth. You'll feel like a new woman."

"Look, Tom, leave me alone and let me get on with the ride. I'm pissed off that there's no cafe stop as it is."

"Sue's realised that we can't be spending the charity's cash on Tuesdays too." I pointed back at my rear panniers. "I've got flasks of tea and coffee and loads of flapjack in there."

She grinned. "I love flapjack, but... how far till we stop?"

"But what?"

"Nowt."

"But your teeth hurt when you bite into it, is that it?"

"Grrr!" And off she went again, so I dropped back and talked to some of the others about non-dental matters.

I'd earmarked a bench and a nice patch of grass with a pretty flowerbed for our drinks and flapjack break, on the corner of a crossroads in the hamlet of Wharles. I wasn't sure how the nearby householders would feel about our Gang of Ten making themselves at home on the nearest thing they had to a village green, but in the event the drizzle which began to fall as soon as we'd filled the paper cups caused a minor crisis which scarcely subsided after I'd opened my front panniers and begun to distribute the matching orange rain jackets which Sue had bought from one of the larger Preston bike shops – at cost price, of course – along with a dozen water bottles and three cages for the bikes which didn't possess them.

"It's only a bit of drizzle," I protested when they huddled together like a bunch of storm-tossed waifs.

"Now it's fucking not," said Gav a moment later, for he'd turned up and had appeared to be enjoying the ride until then, though I suspected he carried a beer or two in his scruffy little knapsack.

"Yes, well, a bit of rain never hurt anyone, and it's a warm day anyway."

"What if it rains on the Scorton ride?" said John, who had managed to stay upright so far.

"Then we get wet," said Sue.

"I'll not go," said Colin.

"But weren't you in the army for years?" I said. "Surely you did much tougher things then."

He grunted and looked away.

"Like long marches and..." Sue trod gently on my toes because, fool that I am, I'd forgotten that Colin's time in the forces, especially his two tours of duty in Iraq, had caused the mental health issues which had subsequently messed up his life. "Well, you don't *have* to go if it rains."

"He bloody well does," said Sue.

"Language," said Cath, before scowling at me again, because my persistence had put her in a tizzy which I hoped Sue would be able to exploit later on.

"I've begun to get sponsors," Sue declared. "And I hope you have too, so none of us can back out on the big day, whatever the weather." She held out her hand and caught a few fat drops. "You must see our wet ride back as part of our preparation."

Moans, groans and mild cursing.

"Then we'll have sandwiches in my house."

Muted murmurs of approval.

"So drink up and we'll be off."

On the way back I told her what a marvellous way she had with her people and how they'd be lost without her.

"Oh, there are other charities in town, some far bigger than ours, so most of them would be all right. I sometimes think I do it mostly for myself anyway."

"How's that?"

She shrugged. "I'd soon get fed up if it didn't gratify me. I suppose in a way it makes me feel fortunate that my life is so much more comfortable than theirs. Who knows why we really do things? Why do you come, for instance?"

"Because you roped me into it. I'm enjoying the challenge, but you'll have noticed that I haven't been to the office to see more of them. I like to see them out on their bikes, not hanging around killing time."

"Well, we do get stuff done there too, but you're right not to come. They associate you with this. Down there you might seem like some of the do-gooders who lend me a hand from time to time. These guys can spot them a mile off, hanging around and getting a weird vicarious sort of pleasure from other folk's hardship. They're often patronising too, without meaning to be."

"Who says that?"

"I do. No, it's far better to play a specific role."

"Yes. I... I suppose we could carry on cycling in the winter months, maybe once a week, when the weather's fit."

She smiled. "I'll leave that up to you, Tom. Oof, my legs are soaked. I'll be glad to get back."

Even Sue's huge kitchen was heaving a while later as we milled around, eating dainty sandwiches, drinking tea and reliving our tremendous nine-mile battle with the elements.

Those whose bikes lacked mudguards had got especially soaked, so Gav, Colin and Ryan's trackie bottoms and socks spent some time in the tumble-dryer. Given Cath's bedraggled condition, Sue had chosen not to exploit her teeth-related tizzy just then, but she did contrive to keep her and Mark there till last, in order to give the latter a pep talk regarding his job prospects before running them home. This was a shrewd move, because although Cath considered herself unemployable, not having worked at all for several years, she couldn't help but apply some of Sue's sound advice to herself.

Sue had drafted several job application letter templates for those of her people who wished to use them. In her latest effort she'd contrived to mention the charity bike ride in order to show, she said, that they didn't spend all their time sat on their bums and twiddling their thumbs. She was modifying this letter for Mark's use when Cath suddenly declared that she was ready to step into the dentist's chair.

"I see," said Sue without ceasing to type.

"Can we go now?"

"Well, I can give Sarah a call, if you like." And to Mark. "Perhaps we should mention our rides in your CV too. We could say you're a group leader or something."

The shy lad guffawed and covered his mouth.

"Go on then, before I change my mind," said Cath.

Sue turned and patted her softly on the cheek. "You won't. Let's see what they say."

Twenty minutes later the four of us were speeding towards Preston centre, still in our cycling gear. After dropping Mark off we made for the surgery, where my wife was waiting in reception.

On spotting a seated patient who was clearly in pain, Cath froze on the spot. "Shit, I'm out of here."

Sarah smiled, took her by the hand, and led her wordlessly into Simon's treatment room.

"Will he just knock her out and set to with the pliers?" I asked Sue.

"I doubt it."

"So will this be on the NHS?"

Sue led me into the tiny staffroom. "No, he doesn't take NHS patients because it would have meant expanding and employing other dentists, or earning less money. He feels a bit guilty about that, so he sometimes charges less and always treats my people for free. He won't do anything to Cath today, but now that she's in his clutches she won't escape. Oh, I'll be so pleased when she gets her new teeth."

I smiled. "Vicarious pleasure, in a good way?"

"Definitely." She bared her own exquisite teeth. "You'll see how Cath gets her act together once she has her new gnashers, and it's largely thanks to you."

"Me?"

"Yes, I'm sure of it. I've been on at her about her teeth for over a year, so it must be something you said or did."

I shrugged and blushed lightly. "Oh, I dunno."

Cath soon stepped out of the room with her mouth clamped resolutely shut, while Simon's grin made his canines twinkle under the bright lights, which reminded me of the day when he'd made up his mind to give me the bike that had relaunched my cycling career.

"Right, you may be a rider short on Friday, as Cath, Sarah and I have a little business to attend to on Thursday evening." He squeezed his patient's arm. "After which I'll drive you home so you can try out your temporary dentures in private."

"Thanks, Simon," she murmured.

Twinkle. "Having all fifteen of them out will be hard on both of us, especially you, but you're a tough lass and it's better to get it done with in one go."

"Yeah, I guess so," she murmured.

"The dentures will be a pain, though you don't have to wear them, and we'll soon fit you out with a superb set that'll change your life, and I mean that, because I've seen it happen many a time. So, I'll see you on Thursday at five." He looked at me. "Do you want a check-up while you're here?"

"His are fine," said Sarah. "He natters so much about cycling these days that I'm tired of seeing them."

One good thing about including non-cycling stuff in a book of this nature is that it diverts the reader away from the fact that describing an endless series of rides can make for a rather tiresome narrative. One good thing about being involved in this kind of project was that it diverted my own mind away from cycling and helped me to put my hobby into perspective. At this time, had I not been helping Sue, I fear I would have spent almost every waking hour reading and watching things about cycling, cycle touring, cycle racing, bikes and related gear, which would have been a truly sad state of affairs for a man of sixty who suddenly had all the time in the world to expand his horizons rather than narrow them.

Having decided that I'd continue to cycle with Sue's people after the sponsored ride if any of them wished to go out during the less clement months, on our subsequent training rides – all more or less dry, thank goodness – I began to ponder on what else I could do to aid those with whom I was beginning to feel a real affinity. Although I was on friendly terms with Gav, Ryan, Wayne and John, they weren't overly receptive when I asked them about themselves and I had no intention of being intrusive. For Mark and Cath, Sue was still very much their guiding star, which left Colin, the ex-soldier, and Danny, who has yet to get a mention but had been in my thoughts from day one.

Like Colin he was older than the others – forty-seven at the time – and he was also still paying the price for something which had happened a long time ago. While Colin was being invalided out of the army in 2006, Danny was in prison, serving the final months of a seven-year sentence for manslaughter. He'd been charged after a routine pub brawl had ended with a drunken opponent banging the back of his head on a corner of the bar and dropping dead on the spot. Danny had shoved the victim, so he took the rap without complaint, little knowing that he'd end up behind bars for so long, partly due to his failure to adapt to conditions inside, thus squandering his chances of an early release. On leaving prison his probation officer had helped him to find a job on a building site, but that and subsequent periods of work rarely lasted for longer than a month, because although the building trade isn't too fussy about criminal records, his apparently ghastly crime made him something of a last resort for the job agencies.

"I got so fed up of being laid off just as I was getting into it that about two years ago I decided not to bother any more," he told me on our second ride to Roots Cafe, an uneventful eighteen-mile outing which Cath had chosen to miss after her anaesthetised three-hour stint in Simon's chair.

"I see. So what now?" I asked the slim, ordinary-looking man who had never taken drugs or drowned his ongoing sorrows in too much drink, which may have been why I admired his quiet stoicism so much.

He shrugged. "I'll just live off the dole and go on as best I can. I mean, I still apply for loads of jobs, but my conviction will never be spent and I refuse to lie about it. It was just a tragic accident. It wasn't even a proper fight, just a tussle, but I ended up with the shitty end of the stick and a bloody crap lawyer. I did get into fights inside, 'cause I wouldn't take any bullying, so I didn't get early release in the end. I studied a fair bit though, but a fat lot of good that's done me."

When he told me he'd achieved some hospitality qualifications and worked in the kitchen towards the end of his sentence I really pricked up my ears.

"So why didn't you go for restaurant or hotel jobs?"

"I did, and still do, but I've never even had an interview. Sue's tried to persuade me to… to forget to mention my conviction, but if I got found out I could end up in hot water."

"Your only conviction?"

"Yeah, apart from the odd speeding ticket, back when I had a car."

I was about to declare that I'd been a hotel manager and still had lots of contacts in the trade, but I decided to consult Sue first, as she'd already warned me that her people's stories and the truth didn't always tally. Later on after they'd all toddled off home she told me she believed that both Danny and Colin were both perfectly employable, but that neither did himself any favours vis-à-vis the job market.

"Colin's proud in a blustering, sometimes childish sort of way, while Danny's pride is of the quieter sort. Neither of them will grovel to get a job and they've got too used to not working, but I'm sure they could function perfectly well in a big hotel kitchen, for instance."

"That's what I've been thinking, but I'm loath to use my contacts if they might let me down. If or when I put someone forward it'll have to be with the certainty that they'll do their best and put up with the usual kidding around that always goes on in a bustling kitchen. If one does well others may be able to follow, but if I sell them a dud, they'll not risk another."

"Hmm, you'd better bide your time and choose your first candidate carefully then."

"All right."

So, after stepping out of the shower that day, instead of flinging open the laptop and drugging myself on yet more cycling-related media, I sent a few friendly emails to former colleagues who were still very much in the game, enquiring after their health and dropping the subtlest of hints that I might be in a position to fill any gaps in their kitchen staff in the not too distant future.

I need a sous-chef right now, Tom, my old pal Rick wrote back straight away from his Blackpool hotel, so I advised him to poach a competent fellow I knew who was working at a run-down sort of place just down the road. That little ruse didn't work out in the end, but my networking had begun in earnest.

18

When the day of the long-awaited sponsored ride arrived the weather was set fair for a pleasant outing to Scorton, where I'd booked several of the patio tables at the non-snobby cafe, because up to a dozen extra riders were expected to join the Gang of Ten, as well as a few motorised followers. As I'd gradually increased the distance of our bi-weekly rides to twenty-six miles it was a foregone conclusion that all the team would easily manage just six more without difficulty, because unlike me they were rarely in a hurry, although our average speed had reached double figures of late. As for me, I'd only ridden my five-mile course once more and on a windy day I'd been happy to dip under fifteen minutes by just two seconds.

That course would always be there for when I fancied a challenge, I told Simon as we freewheeled down a lane over the M6. We were bringing up the rear of our loosely knit peloton which had speeded up slightly on nearing Scorton.

"I set off to do it again the other day, but I just carried on to Cockerham and ended up coming back this way. I averaged over seventeen miles an hour without trying too hard."

He laughed. "Still obsessed by your average speed, but I must say you're doing better than I expected."

"How's that?"

"Well, knowing you as I do, I really feared that you'd succumb to the temptation of racing and end up like him and many others." He pointed ahead at Bob Taylor, who'd come on a vintage Bianchi steel-framed bike and looked far more dignified on such a stylish machine.

"Hmm, you say feared as if racing were necessarily a bad thing."

"Yes, well, maybe I'm biased... in fact I know I am, but I truly believe there's more satisfaction to be had out of cycling for the fun of it than trying to make old legs go unnaturally fast. When I do a ride, including today's, I do it for its own sake and try to enjoy every moment. I usually strive to empty my mind and relish every climb and descent. I look at the views and breathe the clean air and once I get in the zone I'm scarcely aware of what I'm going to do later or the next day."

"Whereas Bob there is probably thinking about his training zones and stuff like that."

"Exactly. For him every ride, even this one, is a means to an end. We're riding to Barnard Castle next weekend, but his will probably revolve around one crucial hour, on the A6 or elsewhere, when he'll batter himself once again, before going home to analyse his data and begin to plan his next very similar race." He shook his head. "But that may be best for Bob. The idea of riding steadily to Barnard Castle and back would probably appal him."

I smiled. "Shall I invite him along?"

"Er, no, because there's a chance he'd come and he'd disturb my peace of mind and... certain thought processes which develop more readily when I'm on the bike."

"I'm intrigued."

"We're almost there. You'd better go on ahead and make sure your team behave themselves."

"Oh, their cafe etiquette is second to none nowadays. The few who can't do without a fag will slip away for a quick smoke, because they know it's not the done thing. Since Sue scrounged some better cycling clothes for them they're starting to fit in more. Twice a week I believe they feel like truly sporty people, though Sue says they're much the same down at the office. Funny that."

"Even Cath?"

"No, not Cath. She's practically given up smoking and started applying properly for jobs, thanks to you."

"God, it was a tough job getting some of those teeth out." We leant our bikes upon a few others. "Let's collar her now."

So we sat at a table with the smiling Cath and the contented Mark. He'd recently started a warehouse job and was pleasing his supervisor who was impressed that he cycled to work at the crack of dawn. Cath's new teeth were gradually bedding in and Simon urged her to wear them all day long.

"I'm trying, Si."

"What a lovely smile," I said, making her no longer quite so pale face blush.

"Give over, Tom."

"If you want to go for a hotel job, just say the word."

She frowned. "I've only ever worked in factories, and never for right long."

"So what? Anyway, it's up to you."

"Yeah, I'll think about it."

On glancing over at Danny and Colin I pondered on my dilemma. I was all set to place Danny in a Preston hotel, but I feared that Colin might let me down due to his sometimes irascible nature. I didn't expect him to chase the chef around with a knife, but the ups and down of kitchen life – lengthy lulls followed by spells of frantic activity – might prove more irksome to him than a steadier sort of job. Ryan the young (former) delinquent, on the other hand, was impressing me with his constancy and I intended to mention hotel work to him during our next outing, because most of the team wished to continue to do our Friday rides at least until the cold weather began. Gav, that unlikeliest of cyclists, had recently experienced an overwhelming urge to possess his own bike, so I was currently searching for an affordable bargain on eBay, as I'd advised Sue to keep the fleet of eight bikes intact, in case any more of her people wished to have a bash.

Towards the end of our meal Sue stood up to say a few words. She thanked us all for our sterling fundraising efforts which had already netted close to £4000. "So let's have a final push to reach that amount. Thanks to you all for coming today, and I'd like to express my special gratitude to Tom, who's trained us up for this ride and given us all lots of good advice about cycling."

The subsequent round of applause made me blush like a ripe tomato. I stood up and muttered that the rides would go on.

"Speak up!" Sarah cried.

I cleared my throat. "Our rides will continue, hopefully with a few new riders, so let's see if we can do another sponsored ride next year and raise even more money for such a worthy cause. Thank you."

As a second ripple of applause abated Simon told me that he knew what I was thinking.

"Ah, yes? What's that then?"

"That we ought to be able to raise a lot more money."

"What a mind-reader you are. Yes, four grand's pretty good, but I can see the potential for raising a far more serious amount, thanks to this online sponsoring business."

"Any ideas?"

"Well, there are loads of sponsored challenges going on all the time, so I think it's a question of capturing folk's imagination. You know, doing something special and getting the word out there. Sarah says that's the way to go, using social media to get a wider audience, but she'll have to take care of that side of things."

"Hmm, I'll have a think and we can discuss it next weekend."

"All right. I believe it's time to go."

"Do you think your riders will make it back all right?"

"Ha! They're becoming finely tuned cycling machines and could do another thirty miles if they had to." I saw Wayne rolling a fag under the table. "I think."

The following Saturday we were getting quite tired as we slogged into a headwind after passing through the pretty limestone village of Keld. Simon had been disinclined to talk much, so I'd soon stopped rambling on about my job-finding efforts, as I guessed he was thinking deeply about something or other. He'd been riding on the drops for a while due to the wind, then he suddenly grasped the tops of the bars and slowed down.

"Isn't it wild up here on this lovely little lane?" he said.

"Yes, it is. I expect we'll start our descent to Barnard Castle soon."

"Hmm, and I think I can hear the traffic from the A66, but all good things must come to an end."

"Er, yes, I guess so."

"Wouldn't it be great to ride for day after day, only passing through small villages, or better still, no villages at all?"

"Yes, but that won't happen in this country, not even in Scotland."

"No, not in this country," he said, before lapsing into silence once more.

As we descended, the open moorland changed to walled pastureland and the hum of traffic put an end to our bucolic idyll in the hills. Barnard Castle was bustling and we soon found the upmarket B&B where Simon and Sue had stayed before. My friend became quite light-hearted as we showered and donned our lightweight glad rags before hitting the town.

"I feel like having a good few drinks tonight," he said as we entered the ancient Old Well Inn on the High Street.

"Yes, but we mustn't overdo it," I said, because Simon was a notorious lightweight where serious drinking was concerned.

Over our meal he told me about the recent Iceland trip in more detail. He and Sue had driven mostly around the coast, sleeping in rather touristy fishing villages and only making the odd sally inland in their hired 4×4.

He sipped his beer and shook his head. "Boy is it wild in the interior of Iceland. It'd be great to cycle straight across, from west to east. There are no towns and few proper roads, so it'd have to be a gravel bike affair with tons of provisions."

"Hmm, yes, it sounds… interesting."

"It'd be less than four hundred miles though." He drank. "I like northern Europe."

"Yes, in summer," I said, having once been on a hotel-related jolly to Stockholm around Christmastime.

"Coffee or more beer?"

"Coffee for me."

"I'm going to retire next May."

"Because tomorrow we've… what?"

"You heard."

My right arm tingled as I downed the rest of my pint. "That's great. A year earlier than you intended."

"That's right."

"Does… no, I won't ask you if Sarah knows, because I'm sure you've discussed it with her."

"We've spoken of little else all week, apart from teeth, of course."

"She kept that quiet. What does she think?"

"She's happy to call it a day too. One year more or less won't affect her splendid pension much at all and... well, I think we're both getting jealous of you and Sue."

"Sue puts in a lot of hours with her people."

"Yes, because she wants to, but Sarah and I feel that we've looked into enough thousands of mouths now."

I chuckled. "Will you keep a chair and enough dental gear to perform a few extractions now and then?" I said, thinking of Sue's people.

"No, in dentistry you can't really do a bit on the side like that, but I'm friendly with an NHS dentist who's promised to take them on."

"That's good."

Our coffees arrived with the brandies which Simon had sneakily ordered.

"I feel a bit guilty about having gone private so long ago."

"Hmm."

He clapped and rubbed his hands together. "But now we're loaded, so we'll be able to help people out as and when we see fit." He sipped his brandy and grinned. "So, Tom, what's our plan for next summer?"

"I... well, this is all a bit sudden. Will you want to come on my thousand-mile charity ride?"

He bit his bottom lip and moved his head from side to side. "Oh, I think we can do better than that."

I gulped. "What, like cross a continent?"

He giggled. "I've been plotting no end of routes on the map, but the other day I hit upon one which might be right up our street."

"It's not… Iceland, is it?"

He swatted the air. "Nah, that's just a week-long ride we can do anytime."

"Yes, anytime."

He sipped his coffee, then his brandy, then he poured a little brandy into his coffee and sipped that. "I propose that next summer we ride from Fulwood to…" He performed a rapid drum-roll on the table. "To… Skarsvåg. What do you think about that, eh?"

"Where the hell's that?"

"Skarsvåg, my boy, is reputed to be the most northerly fishing village in the world."

"Whi… which continent is it in?"

"It's in Norway, of course, well inside the Arctic Circle, which is why we're going in summer, as it might get a bit chilly otherwise."

"And how far is that from home?"

"Oh, not as far as it sounds. If we catch the ferry from Harwich to Holland it's probably no further than 2,500 miles, depending on which way we go. I think we could do that comfortably in about six weeks, then maybe meet the girls up there somewhere and chill out for a while."

"Right. Have you mentioned this to Sarah too?"

"Yes, among other routes, like home to Istanbul and home to Sicily, but we both agree that the Scandinavian journey will be the prettiest and quietest one, and we're unlikely to suffer from the heat." He raised his glass. "To adventure! Cheers."

We clinked and drank.

"So, Tom, are you up for Skarsvåg?"

"Yes, I am."

"Good. As soon as I retire I'll start getting the miles in. How will this great challenge affect your cycling career?"

I shrugged and smiled. "It'll enrich it – greatly, I think – though to be honest I feel pretty enriched by my cycling already."

We drank another toast to our favourite sport, then began to make plans.

AFTERWORD

Thank you for following my journey thus far. At the time of publication the follow-up to this book is just a mass of notes and disconnected passages. If this modest volume is reasonably well-received I shall get down to writing it soon, but at present I find myself in something of a dilemma. Should I describe more thoroughly my ongoing work for Sue's charity, I ask myself, or will the majority of my readers be interested principally in my subsequent trips and other strictly cycling-related material?

If you can spare the time to write a review, either good or bad, I'd appreciate your comments on this matter, as they'll help me to decide how best to proceed.

Thanks again, and happy cycling,

Tom Eastham